COMMONS MUSEUMS

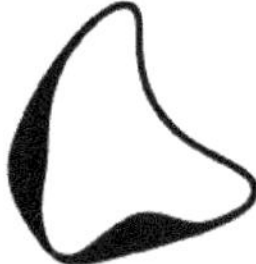

Worlding Public Cultures

This publication series investigates the global dimensions of contemporary public culture through the concept of 'worlding', an understanding of the world generated through continuous processes of world-making. The deployment of 'worlding' in this series builds on the postcolonial project of critiquing universalized Eurocentric frameworks, and is committed to a radical ontology of relationality. Going beyond current top-down models of inclusion, diversity, and other representations of the global, the series critiques radical alterity in favour of a pluriversality attendant to entanglements, difficult histories, and power relations. It grounds the global within local and transculturally/transnationally intertwined worlds, and foregrounds the possibility of continuously making and re-making new worlds through the arts.

COMMONS MUSEUMS
Pedagogies for Taking Ownership of What is Lost

NURAINI JULIASTUTI

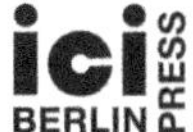

ici BERLIN PRESS

ISBN (Print): 978-3-96558-070-1
ISBN (PDF): 978-3-96558-071-8
ISBN (EPUB): 978-3-96558-072-5

Worlding Public Cultures
ISSN (Print): 2939-9211
ISSN (Online): 2939-922X

Bibliographical Information of the German National Library
The German National Library lists this publication in the Deutsche
Nationalbibliografie (German National Bibliography); detailed
bibliographic information is available online at http://dnb.d-nb.de.

In Europe, the print edition is printed by Lightning Source UK Ltd., Milton
Keynes, UK. See the final page for further details.

The digital edition can be downloaded freely at:
https://doi.org/10.37050/wpc-ca-04.

ICI Berlin Press is an imprint of
ICI gemeinnütziges Institut für Cultural Inquiry Berlin GmbH
Christinenstr. 18/19, Haus 8
D-10119 Berlin
publishing@ici-berlin.org
press.ici-berlin.org

Contents

Note on Names

The standard practice in academic work centred on Indonesia is to cite names as they are used in Indonesia itself. This means using a person's nickname or the first in their series of names, since a last name in Indonesia does not equate with a surname, as in Western naming practices. For example, I use 'Dicky' when referring to Dicky Senda and 'Diah' when referring to 'Diah Widuretno'. It is also common for Indonesians to have one-word names, as in the author Dharmaningtyas, who is referenced in this book.

INTRODUCTION: 'COMMONS MUSEUMS' AS A COUNTER-AUTHORITATIVE FORM OF 'WORLDING'

Sekolah Pagesangan (Pagesangan School) is located in the village of Wintaos on the outskirts of Yogyakarta (Figure 1). It was founded in 2014 by researcher and cultural activist Diah Widuretno with the aim of nurturing the sense of collective resilience embedded in subsistence farming and the community's economy. Its name derives from the Javanese word *gesang*, meaning 'life'. *Pagesangan* thus means 'to live'. Lakoat.Kujawas comprises a library and social enterprise and was founded in 2016 by writer and artist Dicky Senda (Figure 2). It is run by the community in Taiftob Village, North Mollo District, in South Central Timor municipality. Among its activities, it organizes the Skol Tomolok (Tomolok School), which was established to revive local forms of knowledge and develop creative spaces as platforms for communication within the Indigenous Mollo community. In the local Uab Meto language, *lakoat* denotes a native plum that is very similar to the Japanese plum, while *kujawas* means guava — both of which are fruits found in abundance around Mollo.

This case study highlights Pagesangan and Lakoat.Kujawas as examples of initiatives that aspire to achieve self-sustainability by drawing on what is available in their immediate environment — which I will refer to here as 'commons museums'. My conceptualization of commons museums is exploratory; I use it to describe counter-authoritative cultural institutions, as well as a set of strategies for 'worlding' modelled on alternative spaces and community organizations. I draw upon Donna Haraway's concept of 'sympoietic worlding', which refers to the process of becoming with multispecies ordinary beings.[1] According to Haraway, this produces a situation of co-making worlds. Haraway writes that 'It is time to turn to sympoietic worldings, to vital models crafted in SF patterns in each zone, where the ordinary stories, ordinary becoming "involved in each other's lives" propose ways to stay with the trouble in order to nurture the well-being on a damaged planet.'[2] Haraway refers to the ordinary as the stories of non-heroes, which are interconnected with each other in an attempt to get through a critical time. In my research, this provides insights into the definition of 'world-making' practices. In what follows, the meaning of 'worlding' is based on Pagesangan and Lakoat.Kujawas's creative attempts to reset the lives of their communities by tuning into different realities of progress, while simultaneously allowing space for ancestral worldviews to guide their process. This involves developing strategies to create public learning spaces that also function as cultural institutions for the wellbeing of the community. It transforms these spaces into alternative infrastructures for contextual education, archiving, and community economies.

My definition of commons museums stands in contrast to existing understandings of what a museum is and does. In particular, commons museums are not institutions of

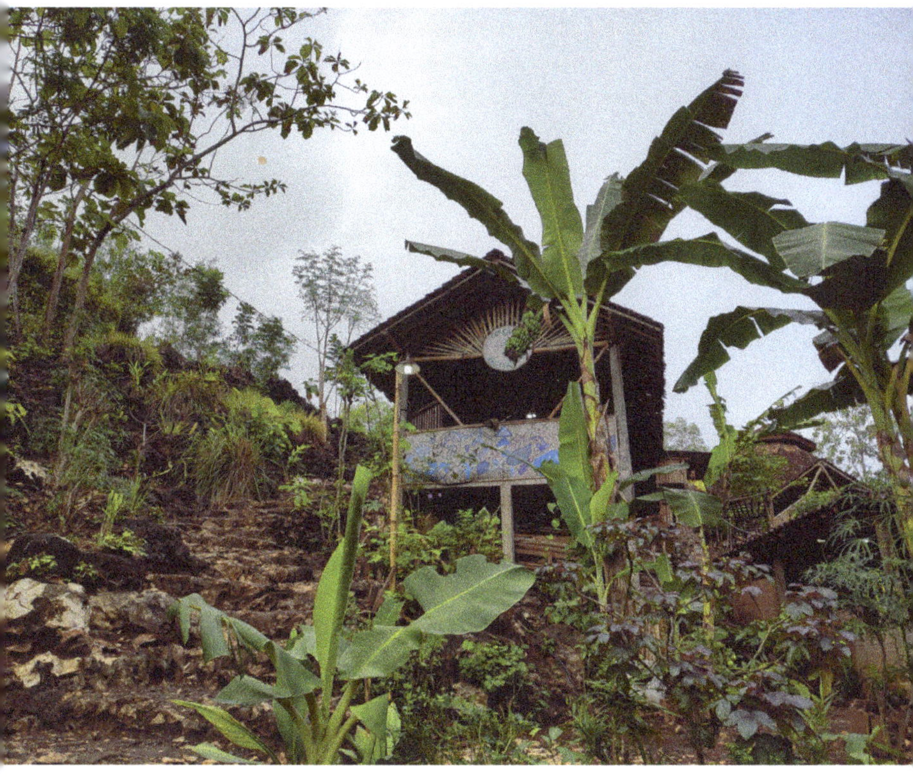

Figure 1. The headquarters of Pagesangan School, 2023, which is comprised of three bamboo and wood constructions and functions as a library and space for gatherings, workshops, and cooking. © Nuraini Juliastuti.

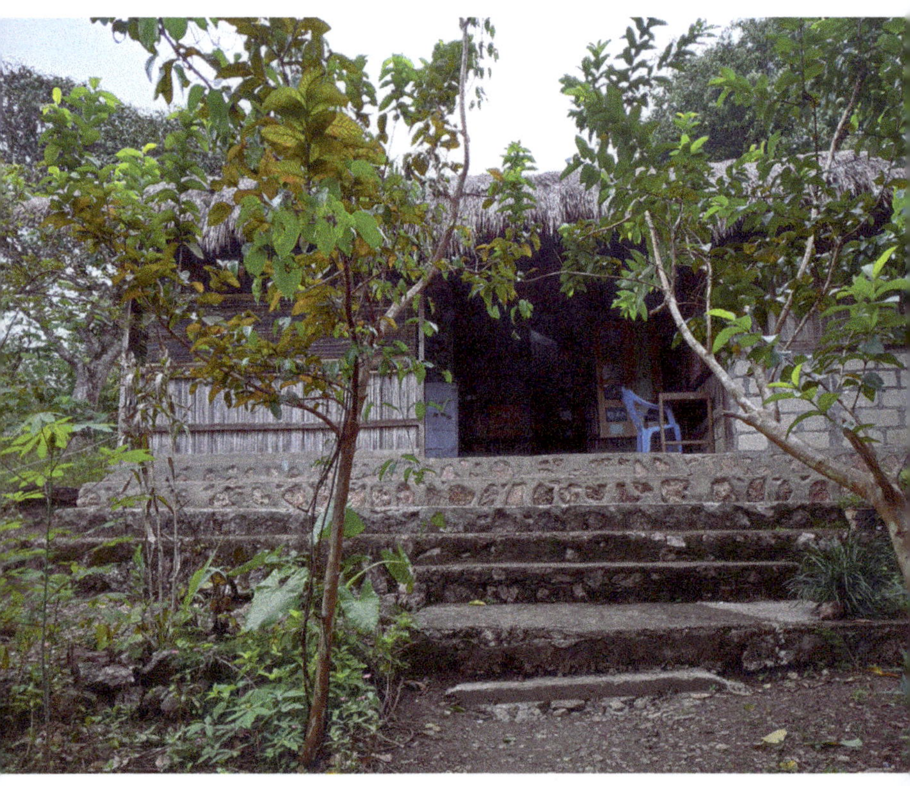

Figure 2. The headquarters of Lakoat.Kujawas, 2023. *Lakoat* and *kujawas* trees grow in front of the library. © Nuraini Juliastuti.

authority, holding privileged positions that influence knowledge and preservation, as well as concepts of legacy and inheritance. Furthermore, commons museums represent an alternative to the grand design of national education, which is often orientated towards productivity, uniform imagination, and undermining the validity of Indigenous knowledge. Instead, the idea of a commons museum offers a theoretical tool for enquiry to explore localized understandings of heritage, memory, futurity, and knowledge-production. Lastly, while Pagesangan and Lakoat.Kujawas may simply be considered village schools or community-based cultural institutions, by referring to them as common museums, I aim to highlight their existence beyond a binary system that separates museums and education. This term, moreover, spotlights how they have transformed alternative spaces into sites where local collective visions meet wide-ranging, ongoing, and contextual politico-economic agendas. These include current discourses around extraction — and being extracted — particularly in relation to discussions around restitution in Museum Studies with regard to Indonesia and other formerly colonized countries.

Over the course of my research, I encountered numerous attempts to redefine what a museum is. The following are the most relevant to this chapbook. Firstly, the Extraordinary General Assembly of the International Council of Museums (ICOM) approved a new definition of a museum in 2022:

> A museum is a not-for-profit, permanent exhibition in the service of society that researches, collects, conserves, interprets and exhibits tangible and intangible heritage. Open to the public, accessible, inclusive, museums foster diversity and sustainability. They operate and communicate ethically, professionally and with the participation of communities, offering varied experiences for education, enjoyment, reflection and knowledge sharing.[3]

Secondly, the confederation of major European museums, art institutions, research centres, and think tanks known as L'Internationale recently launched a project called 'Museum of the Commons' (from 2023 to 2026). This explores current practices and the future of museums *as institutions* via three thematic threads that reflect challenges faced by contemporary societies: 'climate', 'situated organizations', and 'past in the present'. In each thread, the project aims to: confront the climate crisis, seek more active engagement in complex social networks and ecosystems, and mobilize art and culture as tools of healing, reconstruction, and repair within the enduring impact of colonial violence.[4] Although the term commons museums bears a resemblance to the title 'museum of the commons', it should not be mistaken for the same thing. As I will show, commons museums draw on the ethos of collectivizing methodological principles to create balance in knowledge-production by producing archives and knowledges that always evolve along with how communities reimagine what to bequeath in the future.

Both ICOM's new definition of the museum and L'Internationale's 'Museum of the Commons' illustrate the initiatives of global forums that show how knowledge-producers such as museums, research centres, and art and cultural institutions develop their new visions of public-mindedness through active listening to contemporary struggles. While I value these as declarations of solidarity and desire for better futures, these are state-to-state cooperations that always take a long time to materialize into real action. In the meantime, museums and other art and cultural institutions will keep organizing exhibitions in accordance with their own perspectives and mindsets. Pagesangan and Lakoat.Kujawas, however, embody their vision of community and commons-making through sustainable practices with the various beings in their ecosystems.

Over the course of writing this chapbook, I witnessed the intensification of debates around attempts to restitute objects that were stolen during the Dutch colonial period and are now held in various ethnology museums in Indonesia and the Netherlands.[5] Central to this restitution discourse was an attempt to restore a sense of justice. This is a collective feeling that is not static, but keeps undergoing transformations over time. The lack of justice is what Paul Basu refers to as a 'rupture', which sees an act of return as the most appropriate response.[6] He further argues that colonial objects in European museums may be seen as 'object diasporas', capable of opening up 'remittances'[7] for the 'source communities'.[8] Thinking along similar lines,

Clare Harris proposes that ethnographic museums in Europe become 'distributive institutions', working to disperse the museum's collections in digital formats.[9]

In addition to these debates around restitution as gestures of justice through return and remittance, the notion of commons museums adds an expanded perspective; it highlights how community struggles are foregrounded as non-negotiable instruments for taking back parts of communities' histories which have been lost, repressed, and forgotten. For some scholars, such as Nishi Doshi, giving prominence to community struggles has also resulted in advocating for the reinstatement of rematriation practices and recognition of the principles of Indigenous women. According to Doshi, rematriation challenges 'the patriarchal settler colonial concept of justice. It decenters the man as property owner and brings in relations to land, ancestors and the rights of non-human kin'.[10] Unlike repatriation, which focuses on the return of historical objects, rematriation is orientated to 'Returning the Sacred to the Mother'.[11] This process can then lead to the production of knowledge and non-material archives, and by extension, heritage preservation.

The practices of Pagesangan and Lakoat.Kujawas illustrate that historical 'theft' of cultural heritage is also deeply intertwined with the ongoing extraction of substances and natural resources essential for the livelihoods of various communities across Indonesia. Recognizing the workings of commons museums as situated between culture, economy, and ecology requires an engagement that goes far beyond the confines of a museum — an institution that continues to be the focal point of discussions around community engagement. For instance, James Clifford's influential concept of a 'contact perspective' continues to encourage collaboration and inclusion within the confines of the structural limitations and internal agendas of the museum.[12] Responding to this, Ruth Phillips has observed that museum practices have entered into a 'second museum age' in which methods for conducting research, collecting, and conceptualizing public displays are renewed.[13] To illustrate this, Phillips points to the model of the 'collaborative exhibition' accompanied by the development of a 'post-colonial museum ethic' as an example of 'a shift in emphasis from product to process, and a renewed affirmation of the museum as a research site'.[14]

While recognizing such shifts in museum practices, I argue here that the notion of the commons museums broadly aligns itself with Robin Boast's warning that a focus on museums continues to reiterate the inherent asymmetric structures which reproduce modes of 'neocolonial collaboration'.[15] According to Boast, this kind of 'clinical collaboration' in reality meets only the needs of the museum.[16] In contrast, my conceptualization of the term commons museums is not based on the idea of redeeming the centrality of the museum as a knowledge-producer about heritage and futurity. Rather, commons museums are seen as part of developing a vision for doing 'politics from below', or what Charlotte Hess and Elinor Ostrom have described as shifting away from the idea of 'knowledge as resource',[17] towards a recognition that knowledge is a common, collective, and shared set of practices. Building upon Hess and Ostrom, I regard museums as sites for the discovery and accumulation of practices, whose institutional and social parameters need to be reimagined to account for 'knowledge as commons' (or 'information as commons'). In order to understand the making of Pagesangan and Lakoat.Kujawas as the sites for discovery and accumulation practices, the following section narrates the history and current contexts of the organizations.

PAGESANGAN AND LAKOAT.KUJAWAS AS HISTORICAL BODIES

Closer to the Stone, Far Away from the Throne

The village of Wintaos is located in the municipality of Gunung Kidul, part of the Special Region of Yogyakarta Province in central Java. Gunung Kidul is situated within the Gunung Sewu Karst, a location with a specific agricultural climatic character.[18] It is famous for being an arid and barren area, with water scarcity posing a major threat to farming development. People in the area refer to themselves as a group who live *cedhak watu, adoh ratu*, a Javanese phrase that means 'closer to the stone, far away from the throne'. The stone refers to the Karst area. In the context of Gunung Kidul, the throne can refer to the still-ruling Sultanate of Yogyakarta. To be 'far away from the throne' also emphasizes Gunung Kidul's marginal position relative to power.

Gunung Kidul has a poverty rate of almost 18 per cent, the highest in the province.[19] Dharmaningtyas argues that systemic poverty, combined with constant hunger and drought has led to endemic suicides, locally known as *pulung gantung*.[20] Poverty manifests itself in many other forms, such as in the enduring memories of the 1963 famine. That period is also known as the *zaman gaber*, or the *gaber* period.[21] The food crisis stemmed from agricultural failure and an uncontrolled population of rats. Diah Widuretno, the founder of Pagesangan, has observed that the *gaber* period is deeply embedded in the collective memory and trauma of many elders in Wintaos.[22] It engenders deep fear and is probably among the reasons why poverty is avoided in topics of conversation. The experience of living through this period, however, also formed the foundations of a detailed methodology for planning the planting and preservation of food. This planning by local farmers later informed the practices of Pagesangan.

In light of its climatic conditions, Gunung Kidul is characterized by drylands farming, which provides only a small contribution to household incomes (Figure 3).[23] Indeed, the farming system of the drylands is often regarded as mere survival farming, and its products are deemed to be insignificant compared to industrial farming. Despite this reputation, being a farmer in the subsistence farming scheme is the people's main means of sustenance. Diah has observed that the drylands have given rise to specific farming wisdom and a rich knowledge of food technologies.[24] Based on his memories of the *gaber* period, Sahid Susanto has further explained that the drylands have proved to have their own capacities for resilience. Barley and sorghum were lifesavers, as they were able to withstand drought.[25] The Wintaos farmers have a long tradition of polyculture farming, which is known as *campursari* (mixing the essence) or *tumpang sari* (multiple cropping). In everyday conversation, polyculture is also known as *semrawut* or chaotic style, in which farmers sow their various heirloom seeds, as opposed to practicing monoculture farming.[26] Every household was able to fulfil their family's needs by providing everything from food to clothes.

With the introduction in 1975 of the 'Green Revolution', a top-down farming policy that aimed to modernize farming systems through industrialization, subsistence practices underwent significant changes in the village. The Green Revolution was carried out along with the ambitious *Swasembada Pangan* (Food Self-Sufficiency Programme) of President Soeharto who served from 1966 to 1998. This focus on the food programme was tied to the growth of agricultural production as part of the *Rencana Pembangunan Lima Tahun* (Five-Year Development Plan) during the New Order period (from 1967 to 1998).[27] This was implemented as part of the ambitious Mega Rice Project, in which the state attempted to turn the swamps (referred to as unproductive land) in South Kalimantan into one million hectares of paddy fields. Rice was, and still is, the staple source of sustenance in the public imagination. In

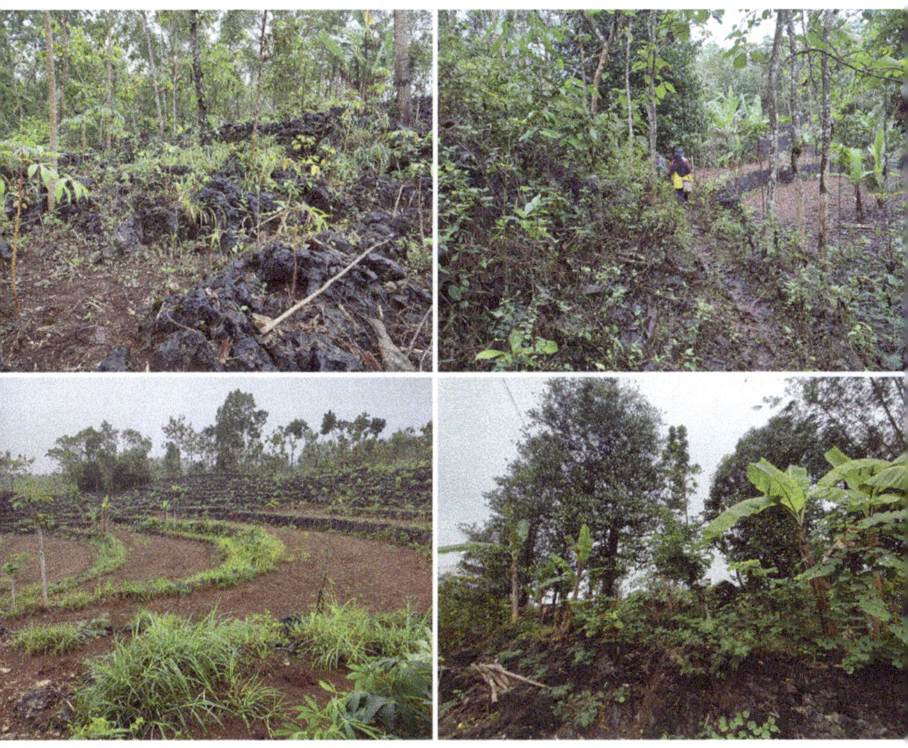

Figure 3. Wintaos's landscapes, 2023. *Menthukan* is the name that refers to rocky plateaus where numerous trees grow, and *lenahan* refers to flat areas where all sorts of plants and seeds grow. © Nuraini Juliastuti.

2020, President Joko Widodo who has served from 2014 to present initiated the Food Estate, the creation of new paddy fields appropriating land in West Kalimantan, Central Kalimantan, East Kalimantan, Maluku, and Papua. The Food Estate is intended to strengthen national food security and national sovereignty, but it disregards the diverse realities of food culture and ignores the history of ecological disaster caused by the Mega Rice Project.[28]

The implementation of the Green Revolution was accompanied by violence. The state made it compulsory to plant a certain quality of seeds, namely IR36 rice. Those who refused were stigmatized as 'anti-development' and 'anti-Pancasila'.[29] Diah observes that the older generation of Wintaos farmers recalled the Green Revolution policy through a 'special operation' known as *Operasi Khusus* (Opsus). Amidst the forced standardization of what to plant, Diah notes that the chaotic and inventive style of farming was lost. She argues that the radical decrease in food diversity necessitated new lifestyles, which affected the subsistence way of living.[30] Villages were no longer seen as resourceful places. The ensuing stigmatization of poverty arising from this period remains to this day. In her book, *Life in the Barren Land* (2020), Diah chronicles the early years of Pagesangan and describes how living in Wintaos taught young members of Pagesangan to predict the future and make important judgments.[31] This sometimes entailed getting stuck with unfortunate decisions, which then put them at a disadvantage. People were taught to consider a limited set of life options such as going to high school, working in a factory in the city, or getting married at a young age. Being a farmer is not perceived as an option that enables a good life.

Water is Blood, Forest is Hair, Soil is Flesh, Stone is Bone

The region of Mollo, home to Lakoat.Kujawas, is located in the South Central Timor municipality, East Nusa Tenggara province. According to Presidential Decree No. 63, East Nusa Tenggara has been classified as an underdeveloped region of Indonesia from 2020 to 2024. All the provinces that belong to this category are known as *daerah* 3T or areas of 3T, the abbreviation of *terdepan, terpencil, tertinggal,* literally 'on the fringe, remote, and left behind'. Situated around Mount Mutis, Mollo has rich biodiversity (Figure 4). This makes the 3T categorization sound ironic. Various problems that occurred in the area are closely tied to the systemic cultural repression of Indigenous communities. The inhabitants of Mollo struggled against marble mining in the 1990s and early 2000s, for which the local government had given permits to various companies. Mass media reports, independent news outlets, academics, and environmental organizations have documented how these mining activities threatened to destroy not only the environment, but also the existence of the clans who live in the area.[32] More than just marble rocks, the stones being mined are known locally as *faut kanaf,* or 'name stones'. This is where Indigenous peoples usually perform the rituals to honour their ancestors. The rituals document the preservation of

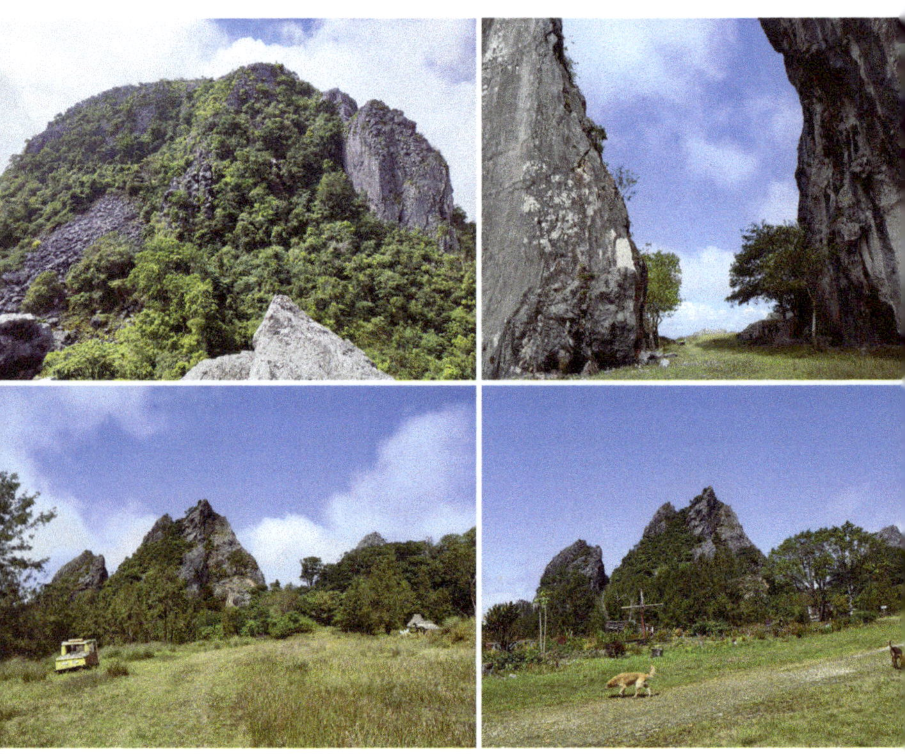

Figure 4. Mount Mutis, 2023. © Nuraini Juliastuti.

the communities' identities, rooted in the natural elements of the surroundings. The local philosophy states that 'water is blood, forest is hair, soil is flesh, stone is bone'. To quarry these stones is thus also to undermine the foundation of their lives.

Resistance to marble mining in Mollo is also often associated with the women's struggle. In the early 2000s, a local resident of the region, Aleta Baun, along with Lodia Oematan and many other women, organized the resistance by occupying Faut Lik, one of the name stones. In order to block the miners (who were backed up by police officers) from entering the area, the protesters did everything they could to protect their sacred space, including physical blockades and face-to-face confrontation. The tactics that were most effective in halting the miners' operations proved to be the women occupying the site with singing and weaving in 2006. The journalist Febriana Firdaus narrated Lodia's account of the events, stating, 'by night, the men would sleep in tents in the cracks of the rock; by day, the women took over the site, singing and weaving.'[33] Woven fabric emerged as a gentle offering to wrap a wound and to protect their name stones. Relearning weaving techniques has been part of the activities in Lakoat.Kujawas (Figure 5).

There is a connection of marble stones that runs through Wintaos and Mollo. Gunung Sewu Karst, which surrounds Wintaos and Mount Mutis, boasts gigantic *faut kanaf* that stand tall around the mountain in Mollo. These areas are believed to be repositories of ancestral

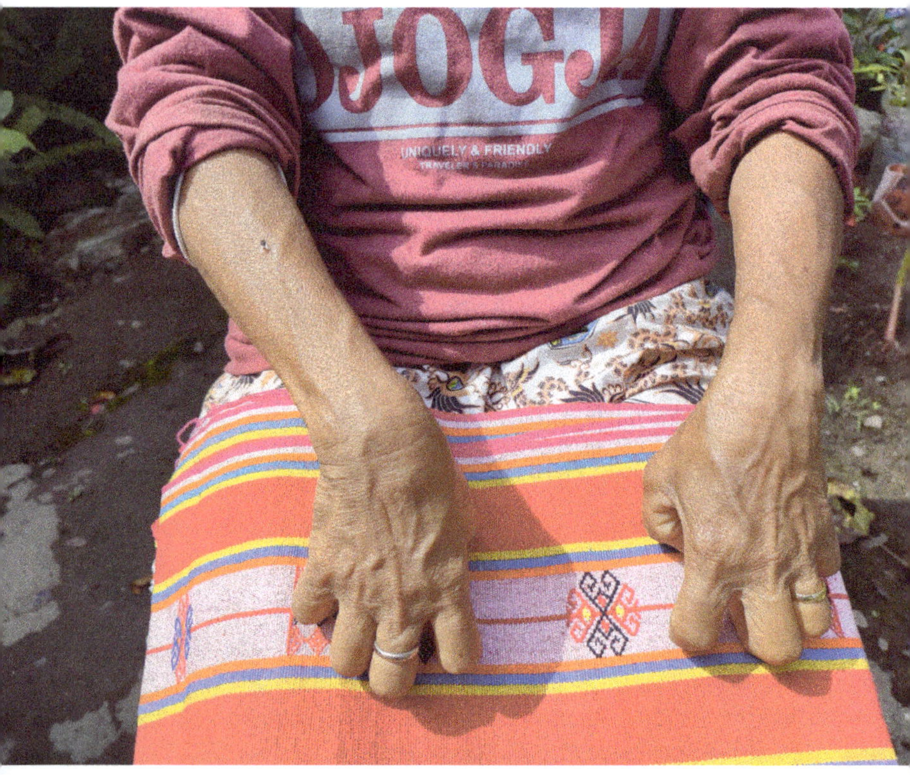

Figure 5. Mama Meti, 2023. Mama Meti is the woman elder in Taiftob Village who teaches weaving in the organization. She has a woven sarong on her lap and her hands mimic the Aus Nobi dog paws pattern of Mollo fabric. © Nuraini Juliastuti.

knowledge and rich in natural resources. And yet, poverty is an endemic underlying problem. South Central Timor, along with Kupang and North Central Timor, are the three municipalities in East Nusa Tenggara province with the highest rate of stunted children in the country — 37.8 per cent.[34] Perhaps because their land is no longer perceived as a sustaining resource, many people feel compelled to become migrant workers. Many of the migrant workers from East Nusa Tenggara enter destination countries through illegal channels, often becoming victims of human trafficking. The number of migrant workers from the province who have lost contact with their families, been deported, or returned to their villages as dead bodies is staggering and continues to make headlines in the media.[35]

Within a context in which development is seen as an indicator of success, Wintaos and Mollo are perceived as underdeveloped and inhabiting marginalized positions. Local peoples stand no chance of being taken into consideration; what is most important is keeping the wheel of development turning under the 'fair' competition of free-market economics. According to Tania Murray Li, when economic competition takes place in contexts such as Wintaos, it produces capitalist relations characterized by unequal ownership of the means of production. Li further observes that the force of competition takes place in 'routine but insidious form'.[36] People feel daily pressure to sell their lands, obtain cash, become migrant workers overseas, or work in factories in neighbouring big cities. Indeed, building a house or buying a motorcycle or mobile phone are also factors that put demands on people. Engagement in many aspects of daily life requires money-based transactions. The economic wheel seems to be defined by the consumption capacities of the villagers. In one of my conversations with Diah, she referred to the consumption-driven life as a globalization problem. In her words, 'the village becomes just like a market. The villagers turn into mere customers, rather than producers, or a group of people whose lives are determined by other people's standards. Along with this, local farming culture becomes endangered.'[37]

DIFFERENT SEASONS AT WORK

Living Amidst Crises

Pagesangan and Lakoat.Kujawas were both founded during Joko Widodo's presidency (from 2014 to present). 'Reformation' was no longer a goal, but rather a new stage in which practices of freedom of expression and sovereignty were simultaneously contested.[38] The post-Reformation period has brought forward multiple senses of awakening where futurity might only mean a locus for a new kind of struggle. The past often comes back in the form of unresolved wounds and trauma; its ghosts inhabit the present. In light of this, I define the temporalities of people in this research as 'seasons'.

Pagesangan and Lakoat.Kujawas are situated within unfulfilled promises and mutated assurances, along with the dynamics of local social and political climates. Their activism is dedicated not to navigating the post-crisis condition, but rather to making sense of a perpetual crisis. During the period of my research, the political situation was characterized by turbulence and unrest. Student activism demanded a revision of the *Komisi Pemberantasan Korupsi* (Commission of Corruption Eradication) bill, the prosecution of governmental elites responsible for environmental destruction, refusal of problematic bills on agrarian and labour affairs, the urgent passing of bills on sexual violence, and the prosecution of human rights violations.[39] Over the course of this same period, I witnessed various agrarian conflicts, many of which led to violent confrontations between Indigenous/rural communities[40] and mining and other companies that have caused environmental damage, often with the backing of the state and military.[41] Nevertheless, people have retained a strong connection with the land and their environments, an enduring relationship that serves as the thread running through the narratives examined in my research. People demonstrate resilience and organize acts of solidarity in order to continue living.[42]

Alternative Spaces and the 'Studying-Turn'

Pagesangan and Lakoat.Kujawas are surrounded by knowledge of the systemic abuse and repression suffered by local peoples at the hands of the state. As Doreen Lee has observed, old and new activists in their time 'lived in a post-Soeharto world without mystery'.[43] This equipped the activists in Pagesangan and Lakoat.Kujawas with the intellectual tools to articulate unresolved issues and formulate necessary actions. I refer to these pedagogical practices as a 'studying-turn'. This comes from my observations of various alternative spaces and independent art and cultural collectives that develop education and learning activities as the basis of their work. For the past eight years, I have observed the rise of different collectives that appropriate the concept of 'school' as a method to critically redefine their relational positions within contemporary social political conditions.[44] This 'studying-turn' operates in two ways: first, it attempts to provide learning spaces for the public. Second, it attempts to reframe certain spaces as studying spaces. I connect studying-turn practices with the rise of alternative spaces in post-Reformation-era Indonesia. Elsewhere, I have argued that 'creating an alternative space has been a habit developed by a new generation of cultural activists in Indonesia as a model platform for fulfilling their visionary ideas'.[45] The existence of Pagesangan and Lakoat.Kujawas demonstrates the making of alternative spaces at the community level, which are derived from the intention to contextualize education within their ongoing struggle. Stefano Harney and Fred Moten situate the act of 'studying' in-between debt and credit. Studying is to stay in debt, which means to commit to social relationships and justice. It needs to be accompanied by a refusal to the powerful accountability system that only seeks control and creates institutional dependence.[46] This also means realizing that 'we owe each other everything'.[47] The studying-turn emerges as a follow-up strategy to reclaim public spaces in post-authoritarian conditions. Taking Harney and Moten's concept of 'undercommons' further, creating alternative spaces is like developing specific study groups, where the activists form infrastructures of alliances for critical thought.[48]

It is important to situate these studying practices within the histories of vernacular pedagogy in local contexts. Soewardi Suryaningrat (also known as Ki Hajar Dewantara) established a local school called Taman Siswa in 1922 in Yogyakarta. The Dutch colonial state perceived Taman Siswa, literally 'the Garden of Students' in Indonesian, as a 'wild' school. Taman Siswa opposed the colonial educational system, which privileged elites.[49] The colonial state also referred to various publications against colonial rule as *batjaan liar*, or 'wild books'.[50] Looking beyond such historical exchanges, within more recent local art contexts, *sanggar* (studios or Arts Groups) have been established as traditional learning spaces where young artists learn under the auspices of a mentor. In my previous research, I elaborated on how the *sanggar* served as spaces to experiment with communal life and a laboratory for developing the notion of *bersama-sama*, or 'togetherness', as a key principle in art practices during the early stage of Indonesian national consciousness from the 1940s to 1950s.[51] Communal life allow students to learn the direction of artistic and social practices from mentors through observing, sensing, and learning by doing. Learning in a *sanggar* is often called *nyantrik*, or apprenticeship. Their informal character put *sanggar* in direct opposition to the modern art education system, which adheres to formal assessment and evaluation.[52] Here, I develop a historical link between *sanggar* and the rise of alternative spaces in post-1998 Indonesia. Alternative spaces emerged as new sites in which to continue the experimental side of *sanggar*. Pedagogy, I argue, becomes the means to develop collective visions in confronting the social environment.

Local Ecology Museum, dimuseumkan

Pagesangan is surrounded by numerous local museums in Yogyakarta. In order to get to the nearest museum in Timor, the people in Taiftob need to go to Kupang, the capital of East Nusa Tenggara province. The local museums of Yogyakarta and East Nusa Tenggara can be grouped into six categories: natural resources,[53] local tradition,[54] colonial war, independence struggles,[55] nation building, and narratives of New Order.[56] These local 'museum-scapes' position themselves as cultural authorities and experts that govern the conventional logic that dictates the types of sites that are to be preserved, the concepts of legacies and inheritance, the idealizations of heroic figures and the representations of entangled narratives of post-colonialism and coloniality.

Post-colonial museums emerged as new sites for the construction of national identity through the official display of what Benedict Anderson calls 'evidence of inheritance'.[57] Anderson referred to museums as *rumah kaca* (glass houses), a term initially coined by Pramoedya Ananta Toer. In Pramoedya's final novel of his 'Buru Quartet' tetralogy, *House of Glass*,[58] the notion of the 'glass house' represents the colonial state maximizing the use of documentation, reports, and archives to obtain total control of the colony, which was bubbling with the beginnings of independence movements. For Anderson, a museum also functions like a glass house; meanings and stories are confined within the limitations of the frames, display cases, and labels. In everyday conversation in Indonesia, there is a popular term, *dimuseumkan*, 'to be museumized', which means to be put in a particular place and abandoned. This popular saying suggests the discrepancy between what is exhibited by museums and what the local public wants to see. Many people who experienced both the New Order regime and the Reform movement are seeking alternative histories and other voices, channels that can reveal what has been concealed or repressed. In light of these examples, I locate Pagesangan and Lakoat.Kujawas within a growing community of history projects.[59] Their existence is in tune with the urge to unlearn the history textbooks, hijack them and find other sources of histories that have been emerging since 1998. It provides insights into what kinds of spaces are appropriate when it comes to facilitating a community's urgent questions.

HOW TO TALK BACK: TRAINING SENSIBILITIES FOR DIVERSE KNOWLEDGE

'Commons People': Designers of a Better Life

The activists of Pagesangan and Lakoat.Kujawas include community organizers, students, artists, scholars, and thinkers. I refer to the activists who run the organizations as 'commons people'. In conceptualizing commons people, I depend on three references. First, Rudolf Mrázek's notion of the 'engineers'[60] who materialized various dreams and plans in the intertwined fields of culture, identity, and nation in the late-colonial Dutch East Indies is instructive in understanding how the people in this research realize their shared dreams and plans through a series of actions. Second, the discussion of key individuals in influential books such as *Figures of Indonesian Modernity* (2009) is useful for identifying the significance of these initiators through their production of the keywords illuminating 'the questions at stake in Indonesia today'.[61] The production of keywords and questions provides a way for the new engineers to contextualize themselves within the social environment. Third, I use Arturo Escobar's notion of 'autonomous design' to think about commons people.[62] Escobar's idea of autonomous design is influenced by the concept of 'autopoiesis' explored by Humberto Maturana and Francisco Varela. Autopoiesis refers to a living system's capacities of self-reproduction and self-organization.[63] For Escobar, designers are the figures who create various tools to reimagine and reconstruct multiple local worlds, the pluriversal condition. Escobar re-conceptualized autopoiesis as a practice of 'changing traditions traditionally'.[64] It refers to a condition where an interconnection takes place through an action to gain independence from within. In autonomous design, autonomy and the community are connected and serve as two principles to guide 'a particular practice and way of thinking about the relation among design, politics, and life'.[65] Autonomous design provides a way to understand how Pagesangan and Lakoat.Kujawas envision new designs for a better life. Their engineering practices include producing, repairing, tinkering, continuing, refusing, and reproducing. They serve as vocabularies of resilience and a dissenting voice of progress. They follow the dynamics of the struggles from within by incorporating voices that emerged from below, within, across, and sideways.

Dicky Senda, the initiator of Lakoat.Kujawas, has referred to the people who manage Lakoat.Kujawas as 'active citizens'.[66] This attribution was inspired by Dicky's participation in the Active Citizens social leadership training programme. Organized by the British Council, this programme aims to facilitate social action plans at the grassroots level. The learning process of 'active citizens' is represented with 'flow' actions. The actions start with the acquisition of self-awareness and the building of relationships with other members of the communities. They conclude with planning social action projects. I observed that Dicky often highlighted his involvement in the programme as an important phase in developing Lakoat.Kujawas. The concept of an 'active citizen' and the fact that it comes from the British Council gives the impression of its top-down nature and a European perspective on what to expect from community participation. It is in contrast with the concept of 'commons people' stemming from the rise of local cultural producers, shaped by multi-historical trajectories. The concept of the 'active citizen' is important in Mollo's context, however. It raises a valuable discussion about the complexity of finding resources to make cultural projects in — and by — the community. I focus on the use of the concept to show how Lakoat.Kujawas actively seeks ways to mirror what transnational non-governmental organizations also do.

To the Lighthouse: The Rise of New Storytellers

Teaching children to read and write, and making that a daily habit, constitutes important activities in Pagesangan and Lakoat.Kujawas. It is worth pointing out that both started their activities by managing local libraries (Figure 6). The building that functions as the headquarters of Pagesangan is referred to as the *guba,* an abbreviation of *gubuk baca,* or reading hut. The libraries are not only an essential source of reading material in the community, as there are also many other activities held in their libraries. This provides insights into the meaning of knowledge: the hidden knowledge learned from villages, as well as the kinds of tools needed to find and embody such knowledge and wisdom.

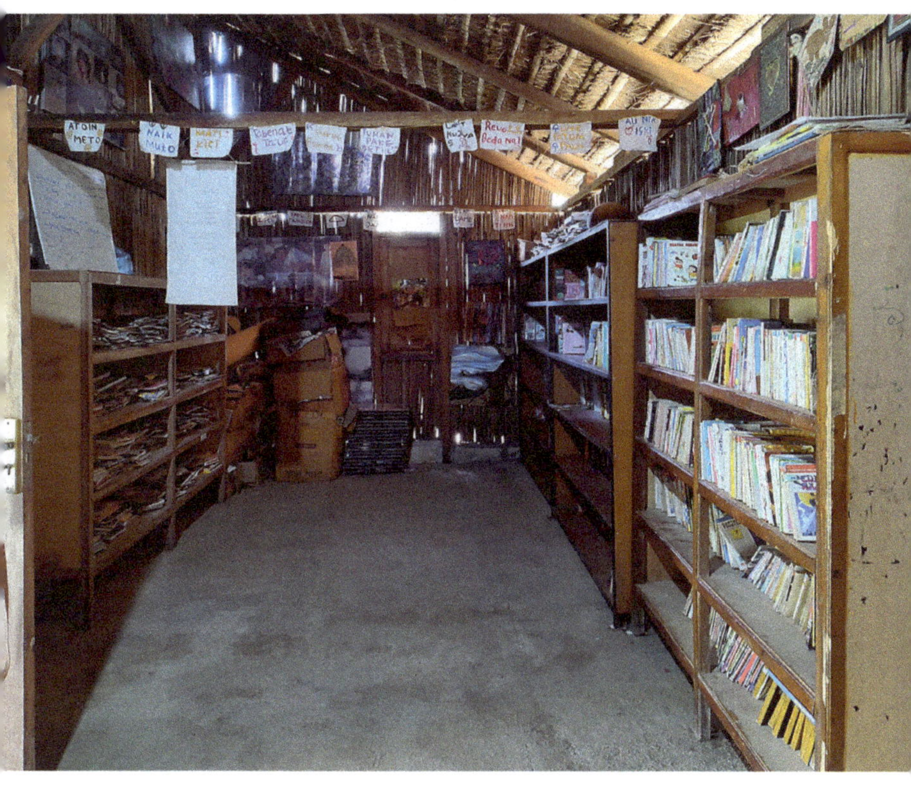

Figure 6. Lakoat.Kujawas's library, the centre of the organization's activities, 2023. © Nuraini Juliastuti.

This section focuses on To the Lighthouse, the writing club in Lakoat.Kujawas that was established in 2017. The name of the club derives from Virginia Woolf's novel of the same title. A more important point in the appropriation of the book's title, however, is the idea of referring to its participants as a beacon of light soaring from the lighthouse in Mollo, a guiding light for those who need it. I situate the existence of the writing club within Lakoat.Kujawas's works in Being and Becoming Indigenous: Kampung Katong (BBI), a network of Indigenous communities in East Nusa Tenggara province. In this network, Lakoat.Kujawas works together with Simpasio Institute (Larantuka) and Videoge (Labuan Bajo). The network serves as the framework for the organization's activities, and the existence of the writing club allows the birth of a new generation of storytellers (Figure 7).

Katherine McKittrick presents her book *Dear Science and Other Stories* as 'a series of stories' and a 'rebellious methodological work of sharing ideas in an unkind world'.[67] Theory, McKittrick argues, can be referred to as 'a form of storytelling'.[68] This question may be extended to ask, what does writing mean for the people of Mollo? In order to answer this, the meaning of writing needs to be expanded beyond books produced and writing workshops organized by Lakoat.Kujawas (Figure 8). Instead, writing is an integral part of the practices used to articulate thoughts and give conceptual frameworks to what they do.

The stories can be divided into two strands. In the first, some of the books produced by the writing club narrate

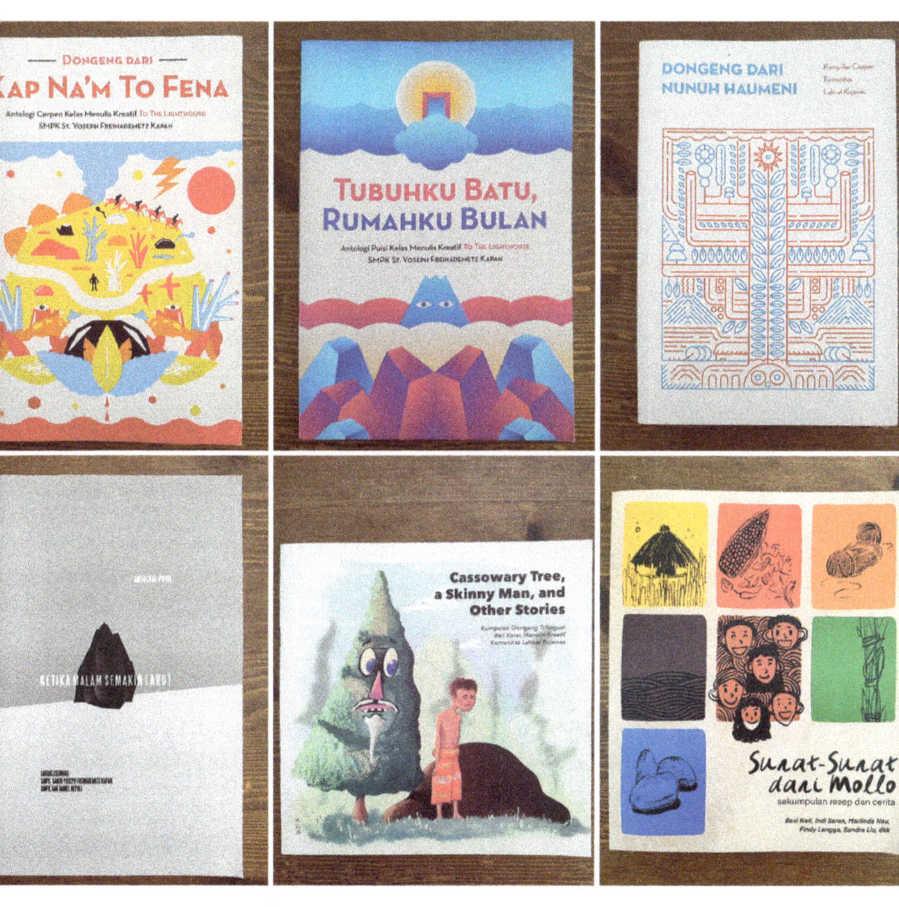

Figure 7. Selection of Lakoat.Kujawas's anthologies of short stories, poems, and folk tales, 2023. From left to right (top row): *Dongeng dari Kap Na'm To Fena* (Folk Tales from Kap Na'm To Fena); *Tubuhku Batu, Rumahku Bulan* (My Body is the Rock, My House is the Moon); *Dongeng Dari Nunuh Haumeni* (Folk Tales from Nunuh Haumeni); (bottom row) *Ketika Malam Semakin Larut* (When the Night Falls); *Cassowary Tree, a Skinny Man, and Other Stories*; *Surat-surat dari Mollo: Sekumpulan Resep dan Cerita* (Letters from Mollo: An Anthology of Recipes and Stories). © Nuraini Juliastuti.

origin stories, with the main theme being how destruction happened due to the disrupted balance between human and non-human beings. The books tell stories of being deeply connected with the environment. Trees can talk to each other and have abilities to convey messages to Usi, the God Spirit, who resides inside the Nunuh tree, the tree of time. Grandma Kaunan, who lives in the Areca tree, can plant water. In Lakoat.Kujawas's latest book, *Letters from Mollo* (2023), participants of the writing club wrote letters to the mountain, soil, stones, stars, moon, forest, water, to the seeds of guava, *bose* corn, and sorghum rice.[69]

In the second strand, participants of the writing club also produce stories about everyday matters. These include sexual violence, domestic abuse, the absence of parents due to their occupations as foreign migrant workers, love, and coming of age. I connect the exploration of these topics with the organization of various activities in which members learn to articulate their thoughts on contemporary social and political issues, including workshops that cover writing about specific opinions, leadership, intimate partners, and domestic violence. Though they are not directly linked to writing, they inform ways for people to position themselves in the ever-changing environment, which always demands new ways of knowing and behaving. Such self-positioning not only goes into the decision-making on what to write, but also requires an act of translation on how to convey the ideas to the community and beyond.

Folk stories collected in the club are referred to as 'oral inheritance'. Formal schools do not provide room for

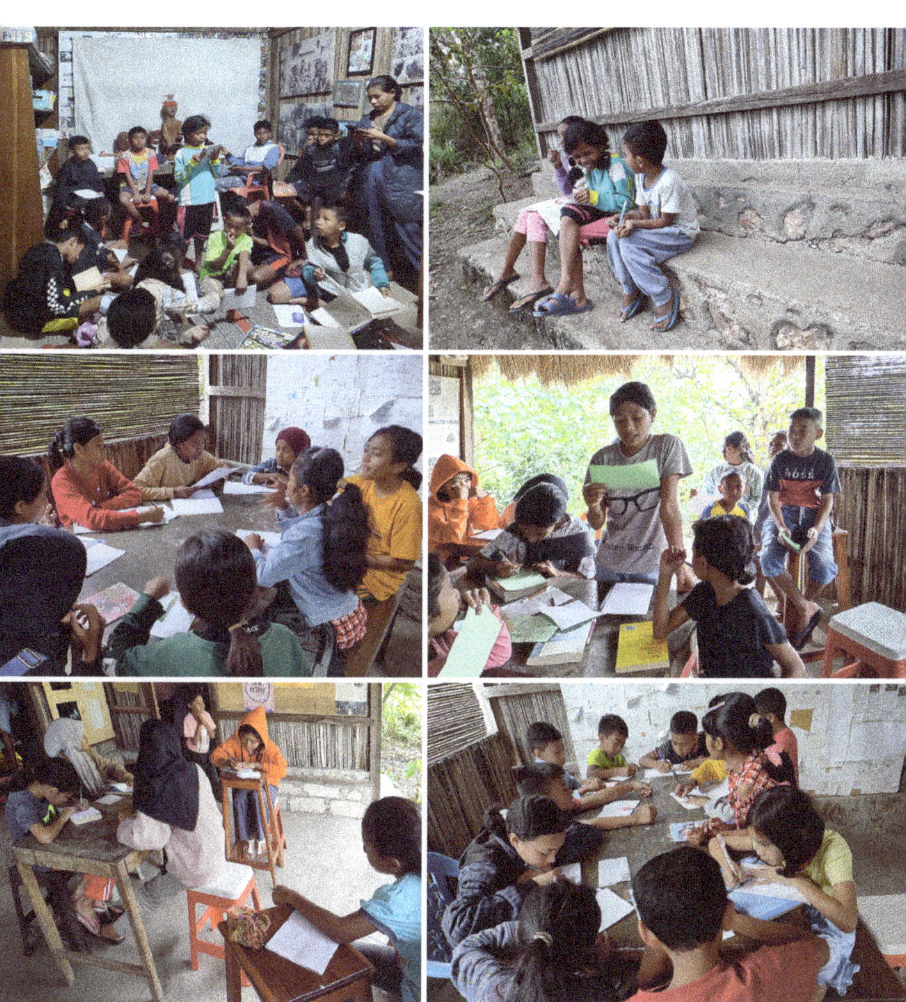

Figure 8. Reading and writing workshop in Lakoat.Kujawas's writing club, 2023. © Nuraini Juliastuti.

local and regional languages, and places in which Indigenous wisdom can be kept alive are shrinking. Due to the fact that the younger generation in Mollo feels detached from their ethnic language, Uab Meto, the translation process from Indonesian to Uab Meto serves as an avenue to strengthen the communication bond between younger and older generations in Mollo. The translation process was conducted collectively by organizing a series of workshops. Some workshop sessions were conducted in collaboration with the Language Unit, Department of Education and Culture, East Nusa Tenggara province. Since translation is a complex process that often reveals the diverse dialects in Uab Meto, the group conducted consultations and multiple rounds of reviews with various groups of elders to reconcile the diversity of translations.

In 2022, the writing club invited various translators and illustrators to work on a special project to help publish an anthology of Mollo's stories in three languages — Indonesian, Uab Meto, and English. Dicky asked me whether I would like to participate in translating some stories. We translated three stories from Indonesian into English — *Cassowary Tree and a Skinny Man*, *Kol Abas and the Hunter*, and *My Childhood Clothing*. Translation work entails a wider understanding of how much is lost and changing in Mollo's social and environmental landscapes, so we checked the translation accuracy of specific words by asking big and small questions: Do Kol Abas birds still fly around the village these days? What does the Kaliandra flower look like?

Being and Becoming Indigenous has developed a series of activities to produce new narratives on the *kampongs* (enclosure or village), documenting traditional medicine and classes on reading the land and Indigenous astrologies. Walking around the villages, or observing what is around them, are meaningful activities where members collect narratives about water, clans, mountains, and fables. These activities allow the young members of Lakoat.Kujawas to have various encounters with elders. The parents and the elders emerged as knowledge bearers to provide contexts for everything that had been lost, for everything that had been disconnected from the everyday. In different ways, each activity shows the routes that are needed to identify all the missing links in the intergenerational learning process. They pursue creative avenues to enable moving back and forth between stories, histories, and artistic expression.

Food Lab and Seed Archives: On Poverty and Making Lists of Abundance

Uem Fatumfaun is a new Lakoat.Kujawas endeavour to create a food lab and seed archives in Mollo. It is envisaged as a space for sharing Indigenous knowledge, archiving local seeds, and experimenting with village food and farming capacities. In developing Uem Fatumfaun, Lakoat.Kujawas develops mechanisms to show the abundance in their environment and to make use of their own resources. I connect the existence of the food lab and seed archives with the stigma of poverty and chronic stunting among children in

Mollo. The vitality of the land and people are exhausted — both literally and figuratively. Food emerged as an area of exploration to deal with marginalization and the feeling of being left behind. The words 'lab'/'laboratory' and 'archives' in 'Uem Fatumfaun: Food Lab and Seed Archives' indicate an intention to institute experimental and caring elements (Figure 9). During Sukarno's presidency (from 1945 to 1967), the crisis was described as the result of population growth and the minimal utilization of diverse food resources. To overcome this, *Lembaga Teknologi Makanan* (Institute of Food Technology) and the Ministry of Agriculture embarked on a major programme in 1960, aimed at developing public consciousness of the existing food diversity. The design of the programme was innovative and centred on the publication of *Mustika Rasa*, a cookbook that simultaneously served as a policy paper, a statement, and a way of encouraging people to deal with the food crisis collectively.[70] The programme endorsed self-reliance as the main principle of national politics on food. In this context, *swasembada beras* (rice self-sufficiency) was transformed into *swasembada bahan makanan* (food self-sufficiency).[71]

The politics of self-reliance is also known as *berdikari*, an abbreviation of *berdiri di atas kaki sendiri*, to stand on one's own feet. The application of *berdikari*, Amiruddin Al Rahab asserts, was part of the nation's attempt to create a strong national economy during the early period of an independent Indonesia. The strength of the foundation lies not only in the potential of Indonesian natural resources, but also in a willingness to focus on the social welfare of people,

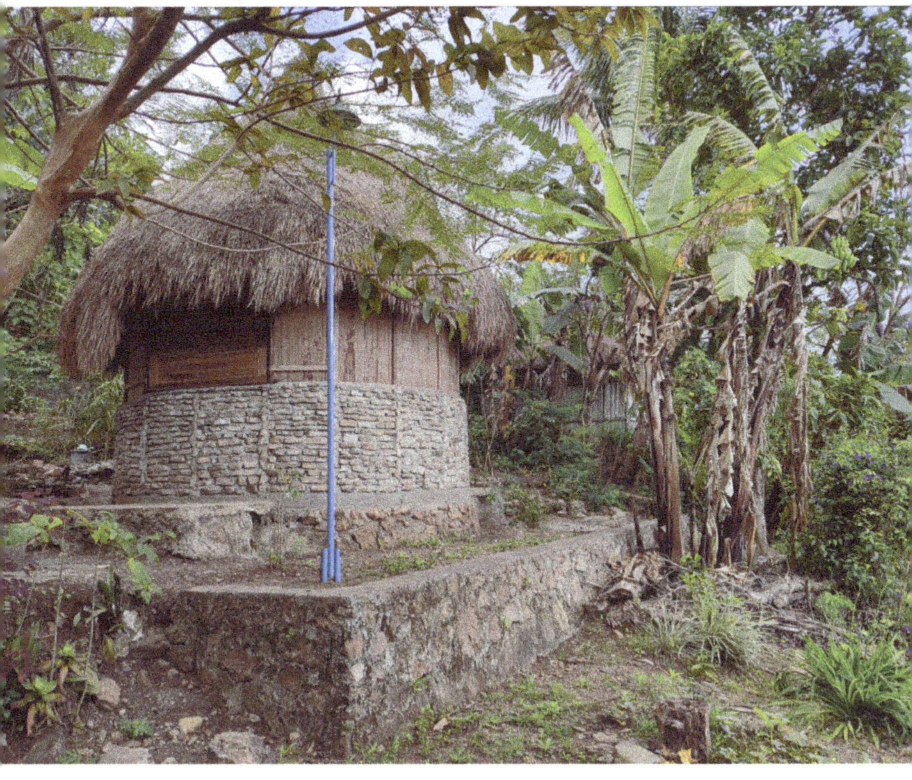

Figure 9. Uem Fatumfaun Food Lab and Seed Archives, 2023. The construction is shaped like an *uem bubu,* the traditional round house in Timor. © Nuraini Juliastuti.

and not to be dictated by foreign economic powers.[72] *Mustika Rasa* was officially published in 1967, the same period as when Sukarno was stripped of power and Soeharto's New Order began. The food resilience programme was abolished, and its cookbook forgotten.

It is important to juxtapose the element of abundance embedded in Sukarno's vision of food resilience and Lakoat.Kujawas's food lab and seed archives with the limitations of seeing rice as a symbol of dominance, uniformity, and the power of state authorities. Abundance is a key concept to activate as a tool to challenge and redefine the meaning of poverty and vitality. Lakoat.Kujawas uses various social media platforms — Instagram, YouTube, and TikTok — to make visible their practices and research agendas. In the context of the food lab and seed archives, photos and videos emerged as a way to build awareness among young people that they are surrounded by the resourcefulness of the village. They also produced a list of abundant agricultural products. As Anna Tsing has theorized, list-making as practised among Indigenous communities serves as 'a self-conscious project of placing a local niche within a global imagining. The lists acknowledged and acclaimed global biodiversity by conserving a local space within it'.[73] In observing Indigenous list-making practices, Tsing suggests reflecting on knowledge as a product of the categorization system by observing the inclusion and exclusion that occurred in the process. The list feels kaleidoscopic and seasonal at once; it can be transformed into the Mollo Seasons and Harvest Calendar (Figures 10a and 10b).

There is a sense of pride that derives from the ability to tell multi-layered stories from the act of list-making. Mollo people's knowledge of plants and food depends on the women and elders in the village. Through their regular residency programme, learning about food and plants is transformed into an open and collective process. Vernacular food knowledge is obtained by walking together and collecting stories, with no fixed system to guide the process. Many parts of the process are built up piecemeal. Yet, instead of considering this as merely an unsystematic process, it suggests the intention of progressing this over the long-term. Enthusiasm is shown by everyone who is involved along the way. The economic value of abundance is demonstrated by the community showing how they can live well in accordance with everything that is around them.

Participatory Research on Edible Plants and Study of Gunung Kidul

The Riset Partisipasi Tanaman Pangan (RPTP), or Participatory Research on Edible Plants, is a project aimed at documenting edible plants around Wintaos. Pagesangan also organizes Sinau Tetanen Gunung Kidul (STG), or Study of the Gunung Kidul Farming System — a course that aims to develop a systematic mechanism where the younger generation can learn about the philosophy of the Gunung Kidul farming system. To follow the local fondness for abbreviations, I will refer to these activities as RPTP and STG. It is

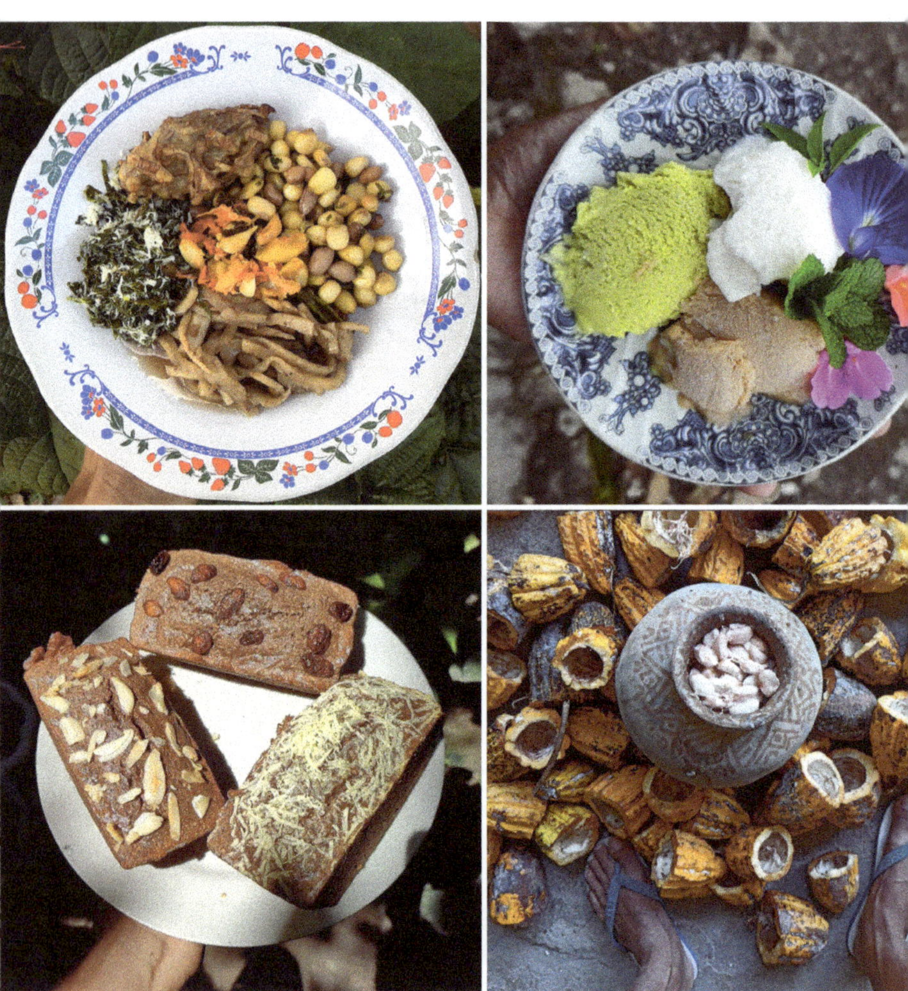

Figure 10a. List of abundance in Mollo, 2021. From left to right (top row): *Katemak* corn, sautéed bamboo shoots in black-bean sauce, cassava leaf salad with spiced grated coconut, banana heart fritter, avocado, lakoat, and soursop ice cream; (bottom row) Noebesi chocolate brownies topped with shredded cheese, raisins, and walnuts; Timorese cacao. Courtesy of Dicky Senda and Lakoat.Kujawas.

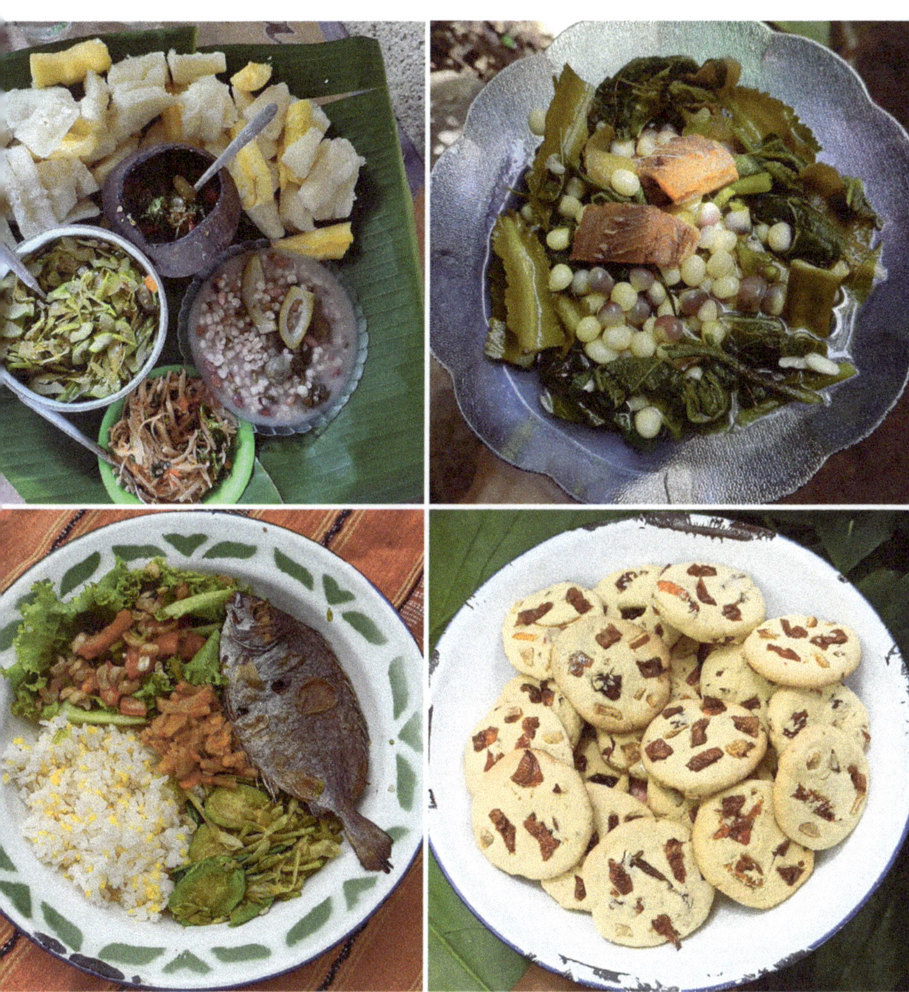

Figure 10b. List of abundance in Mollo, 2021. From left to right (top row): yellow and white cassava, sautéed papaya flowers, bose corn with papaya, red bean stew, wild eggplant, and bamboo shoot sambal; white and purple katemak corn with various greens: kecipir, pempung pumpkin, string beans, kemangi, and caraway; (bottom row) corn rice, Cara fish, sautéed papaya flowers, lettuce, peanut serundeng; mocaf flour cookies with dried fruits. Courtesy of Dicky Senda and Lakoat.Kujawas.

important to note that both Lakoat.Kujawas and Pagesangan design their activities to cater to people from different age groups. This suggests the intention of developing the conditions for learning from each other. RPTP is designed as a children's activity, and STG as an activity for adults. Pagesangan also organizes various activities for the women's group in the village.

In what follows, I examine the practice of organizing workshops as the main format of these activities. Workshops allow for the constant movement between theory and practice. In the context of RPTP and STG, study is emphasized as a mechanism for reconnecting with village knowledge. Pagesangan took great pride in STG because it is perceived as an activity that nurtures a new generation of farmers. In both programmes, participants acted as young researchers and village explorers. From April to May 2021, Diah invited me to join a series of planning meetings to prepare the organization of RPTP. An agrarian activist, Baning Prihatmoko, was part of the organizing committee. Baning also served as one of the tutors in the STG course. According to Diah, Pagesangan focuses on the millennial generation, which has become disengaged from farming culture. RPTP and STG serve as part of a pedagogical model that creates a feeling of being more grounded, relevant, and connected to the village environment. Diah hoped that this would keep young people away from their mobile phones and other gadgets, even just temporarily. In addition, the programmes would establish the position of Wintaos as a source of learning for a wider public. The main implementation strategy in organizing these learning activities was to reintroduce local food systems, ranging from production to distribution and consumption. The emphasis in STG is to teach younger generations that part of the injustice and shrinkage of land is due to the mass industrialization and development policies of the state. Each session in STG is dedicated to learning farming the Gunung Kidul way — how to graft fruit plants, manage dry land, and arrange stones to prepare the rice field in the drylands. Learning how to farm means learning the resilience that Wintaos farmers gain from respecting the strong character of Gunung Kidul fields.

One of Pagesangan's learning philosophies is *sinau kanthi bungah* — a Javanese phrase that means 'learning with joy'. I want to extend the definition of joyful learning as a freestyle kind of learning that is not confined within structured activities. I connect this with the daily activities of Pagesangan members: making *wayang* (traditional puppets) from used cardboard, collecting interesting leaves and flowers for the herbarium, cleaning up the space, making lunch or afternoon snacks, or just hanging out together. In a conventional school, this might be described as playing. These are the kinds of activities, however, that make children's time together more meaningful. During RPTP, children walked around the village, observed what was in their surroundings, interviewed family members or neighbours, and made notes in their journals (Figures 11a and 11b). They learned to listen and ask important questions

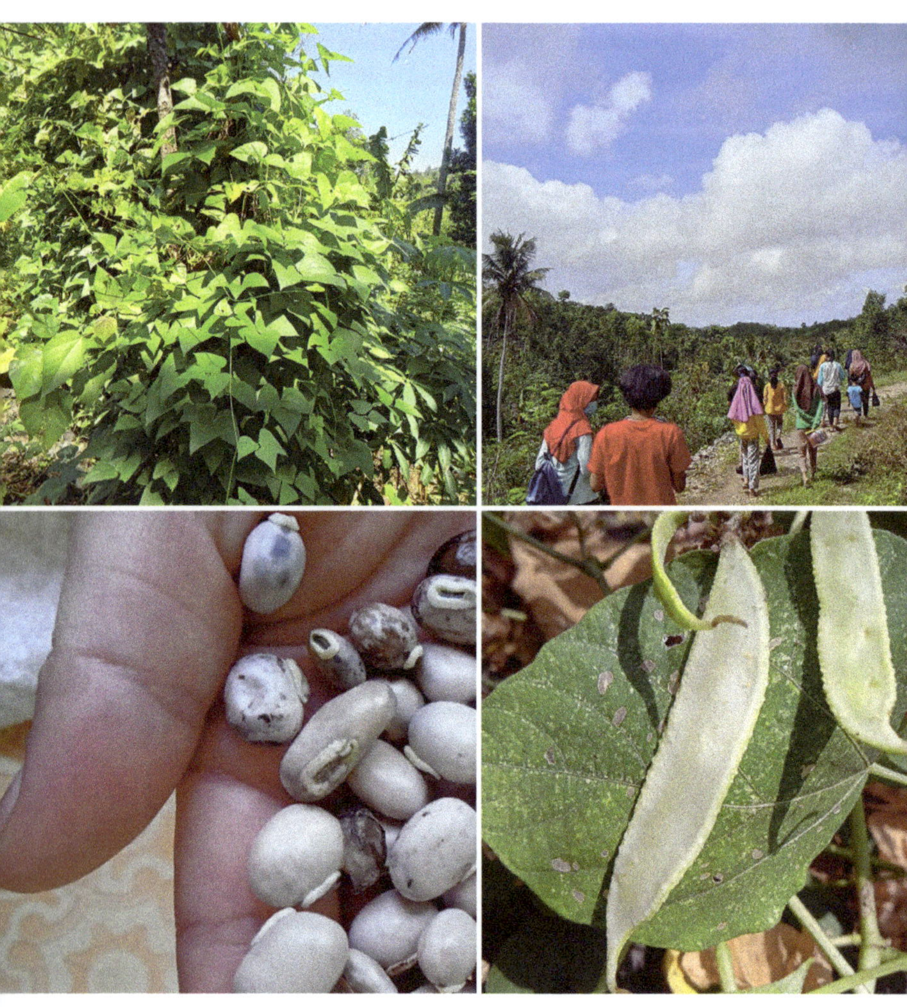

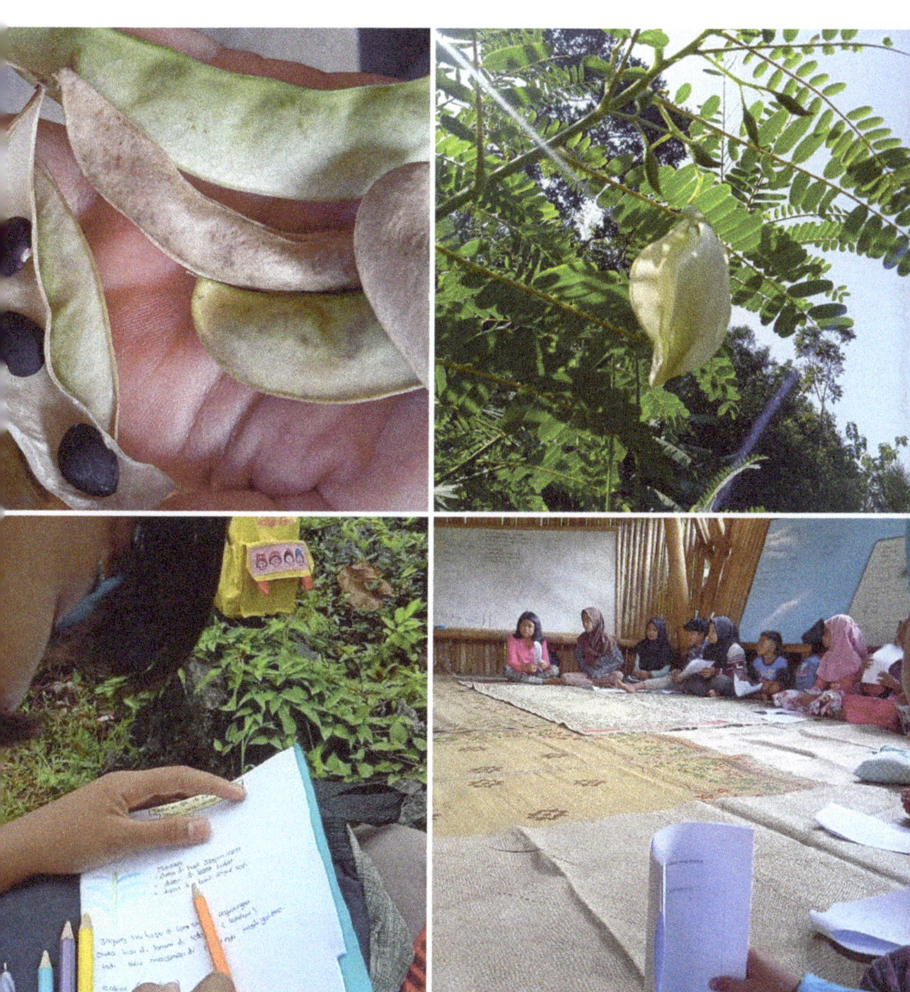

Figures 11a and 11b. Activities in the Participatory Research on Edible Plants, 2021. Courtesy of Pagesangan School.

driven by their curiosity. The following instructions were given on how to draw and write stories during RPTP:

- Draw and describe parts of the plants that you observe (roots, stems, leaves, fruits, flowers).

- Tell stories about the usefulness of the plants (daily food, medicinal plants, or fodder).

- Describe the recipes for how to cook the plants.

- Where do these plants grow and how to plant them?

- Can you tell stories about the seasonal changes during the sowing season?

They produce a list of findings that can be read as 'local Wintaos food knowledge'.[74] As depicted in Figure 12, the list might initially appear to be unfinished or incomplete. Many plants are not yet accompanied by their scientific Latin names, and the column with the researchers' names remains empty. Yet, rather than seeing the list as unfinished, it could be seen to suggest a collective project that is still in progress.

All the plant names on the list are written in a combination of Indonesian and Javanese, to acknowledge how local people in Wintaos usually refer to the plants. In one of the conversations, Baning suggested that the lists should retain local ways of naming. This resonates with Tsing's proposal to see list-making as a 'self-conscious project' to niche a local conservation project within a global biodiversity project. The plants are ordinary and can be found easily

Nama Tanaman	Peneliti	Keterangan (Nama latin ; family ; info lain)
Telo Giren		*Manihot esculenta*
Telo Martapura		*Manihot esculenta*
Telo Brambangan		*Manihot esculenta*
Telo Genjah		*Manihot esculenta*
Telo Kirik		*Manihot esculenta*
Telo Uncek		*Manihot esculenta*
Telo Saeko		*Manihot esculenta*
Telo Kapur		*Manihot esculenta*
Telo Pandesi		*Manihot esculenta*
Telo Mandela		*Manihot esculenta*
Telo Meni		*Manihot esculenta*
Kimpul /Tales		*Xanthosoma sagitafolium*
Telo Pendem (ubi)		*Ipomoea batatas*
Uwi Putih		*Discorea alata*
Uwi Ungu		*Discorea alata*
Gembili		*Dioscorea esculenta*
Garut		*Maranta arundinacea*
Mondro (Ganyong) putih		*Canna discolor*
Modro (Ganyong) merah		*Canna discolor*
Gadung		*Dioscorea hispida*
Suweg		*Amorphophallus paeoniifolius*
Sente (Bira)		*Alocasia macrorrhizos*
Porang (iles-iles)		*Amorphophallus muelleri*
Padi Segreng		*Oryza sativa* (Pari endhek)
Padi Puthu		*Oryza sativa* (Pari dhuwur)
Jagung Putih (tengahan)		*Zea mays*
Sorghum (Chantel)		*Shorgum bicolor*
Jali-Jali		*Coix-lacrima jobi*
Jawut (Jewawut)		*Setaria italica*
Ketan putih		*Oryza sativa* L. var *glutinosa*
Ketan hitam		*Oryza sativa* L. var *glutinosa*
Koro pedang biji putih		*Canavalia ensiformis* leguminoasae/(fabacea)/polong-polongan
Koro pedang biji merah		*Canavalia gladiate* (fabacea)/polong-polongan
Koro uceng		*Phaseolus lunatus* (fabacea)/polong-polongan

Nama Tanaman	Peneliti	Keterangan (Nama latin ; family ; info lain)
Koro enak/sayur (Komak)		*Lablab purpureus* (fabacea)/polong-polongan
Koro pahit		
Koro benguk		*Mucuna pruriens* (fabacea)/polong-polongan
Gude		*Cajanus cajan*/fabacea /leguminosae
Kacang hijau		*Vigna radiate* /fabacea/polong-polongan/leguminosae
Kacang tunggak/tolo		*Vigna unguiculata*/fabacea/leguminosae
Kacang endel		*Vigna umbrelata*/fabacea/leguminosae
Kacang tanah		*Arachis hipogaea*/fabacea/leguminosae
Turi putih		*Sesbania grandiflora*/fabacea/leguminosae
Turi merah		*Sesbania grandiflora*/fabacea/leguminosae
Telang		*Clitoria ternatea*/fabacea/leguminosae
Tayuman (kupu-kupu)		*Bauhinia purpurea*/fabacea/leguminosae
Kedelai hitam		*Glycine soja*/fabacea/leguminosae
Kacang panjang		*Vigna unguiculata sesquipedalis*/fabacea
Kecipir		*Psophocarpus tetragonolobus*/fabacea
Mlanding		*Leucaena leucocephala*/fabacea
Lamtoro		*Leucaena leucocephala*/fabacea
Pete		*Parkia speciosa*/fabacea
Jengkol		*Archidendron pauciflorum*/fabacea
Bayam		
Kenikir		
Kemangi		
Kangkung		
Daun Singkong karet		
Daun singkong sayur		
Gedi		
Kelor		
Daun papaya dan kembang grandel		
Kluweh		
Daun waluh		
Pare		
Pare ulo		
Gambas		
Katu		
Terong bulat (hijau, putih, ungu)		*Solanium nigrum* L.
Terong ungu		*Solanum melangena* (solanase)
Cokak		
Leunca		
Terong hijau		

Figure 12. List of findings of the Participatory Research on Edible Plants, 2021. Courtesy of Pagesangan School.

around the village. The participants, however, often do not know what these plants are called and whether or not they are edible. In many cases, knowledge about the names and usefulness of the plants is confined to the older generations in Wintaos. As such, knowledge of the plants is disappearing alongside the departure of these older generations. By participating in RPTP, participants learn to identify the plants in their surroundings and detect the signs of their disappearance.

Pagesangan Health Store: In Pursuit of a Good Life and Community Support System

Kedai Sehat Pagesangan, or the Pagesangan Health Store, is a social enterprise that serves as the Pagesangan's support system. The health store sells local food and agricultural produce, and has managed to build a good reputation as an initiative to preserve local food traditions. Kedai Sehat is the place to find fresh homemade Wintaos specialities (Figures 13a and 13b). While the shop is managed online through their Instagram handle @kedaisehatpagesangan, it is also a regular participant in various organic and farmers markets in Yogyakarta. This means that Kedai Sehat was well connected to the developing networks of organic health stores, health food bulk stores, catering owners, and food enthusiasts. It also contextualizes Pagesangan within the wider discourse of food literacy and sustainable food practices.

Entrepreneurship paves the way for the development of new areas of study. It functions as an open space to learn about the potentials of villages, the history of farming culture, food systems, subsistence farming, traditional survival techniques, business, and management planning. Kedai Sehat is a small-scale enterprise designed to tackle the problem of how to survive in the village. It is envisaged as a sustaining work opportunity; a long-term outlet that young people can use to survive without having to leave Wintaos. As business progresses, many women are beginning to see its potential to help them obtain additional income for their families. Kedai Sehat serves as a self-empowerment tool for the villagers, and also helps sell agricultural produce planted by farmers in and around Wintaos. More than a store, Kedai Sehat also emerged as a community where the members are constantly discussing different ways to live well together. It is not limited to selling food and produce, but also organizes collective pots (of money and livestock) and takes an active role as a bridge to knowledge about local food and farming.

The relation between Kedai Sehat and pedagogy lies in the opportunity enabled by the members of Pagesangan to learn about the disappearing sources of food. Kedai Sehat created various cluster activities themed around local food culture. The members learn how to make *thiwul*, cassava pearls made from *gaplek* (dried cassava shreds). In this activity, the children learn how to ground, sift, steam, and dry *gaplek*. Children go to see *pasucen*, a Javanese word used in Wintaos to refer to a *lumbung* (barn) (Figure 14).

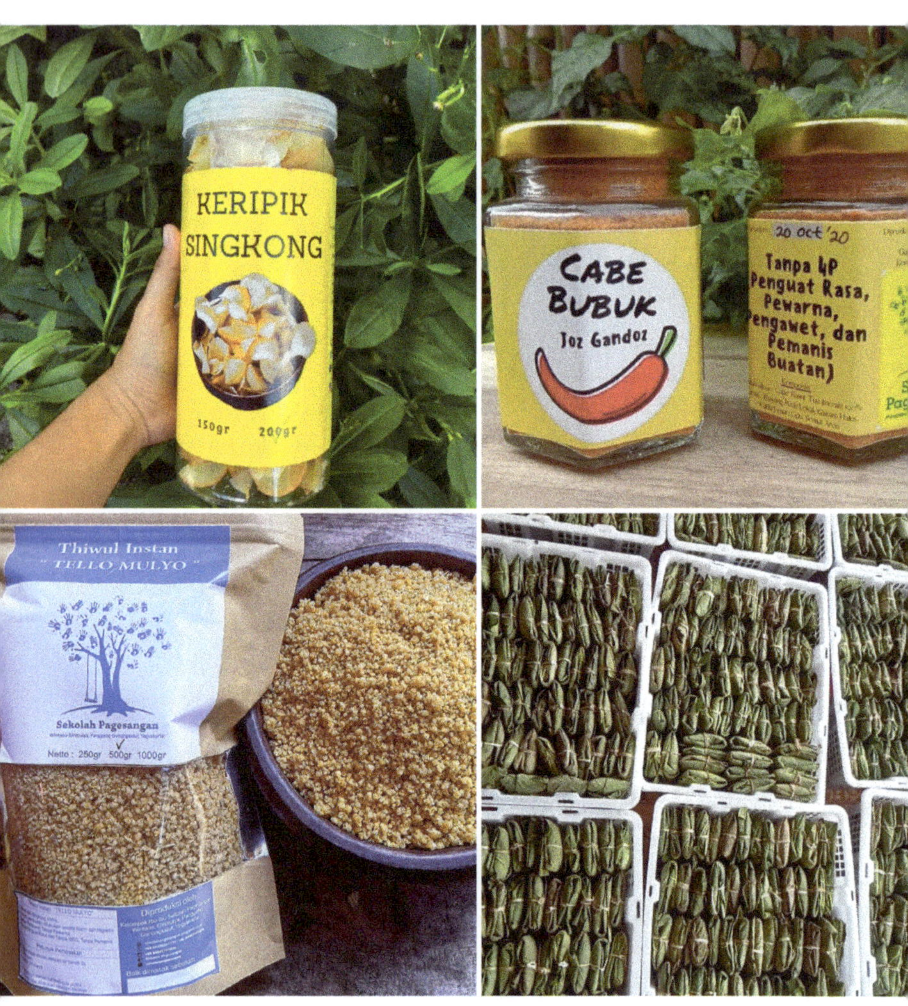

Figure 13a. Products of the Pagesangan Health Store, 2023. From left to right (top row): *keripik singkong* (cassava chips); *cabe bubuk* (chili powder); (bottom row) *thiwul instan* (instant cassava pearls); *tempe* (traditional fermented soybean cakes). Courtesy of Lifia Nuryati (Pagesangan School).

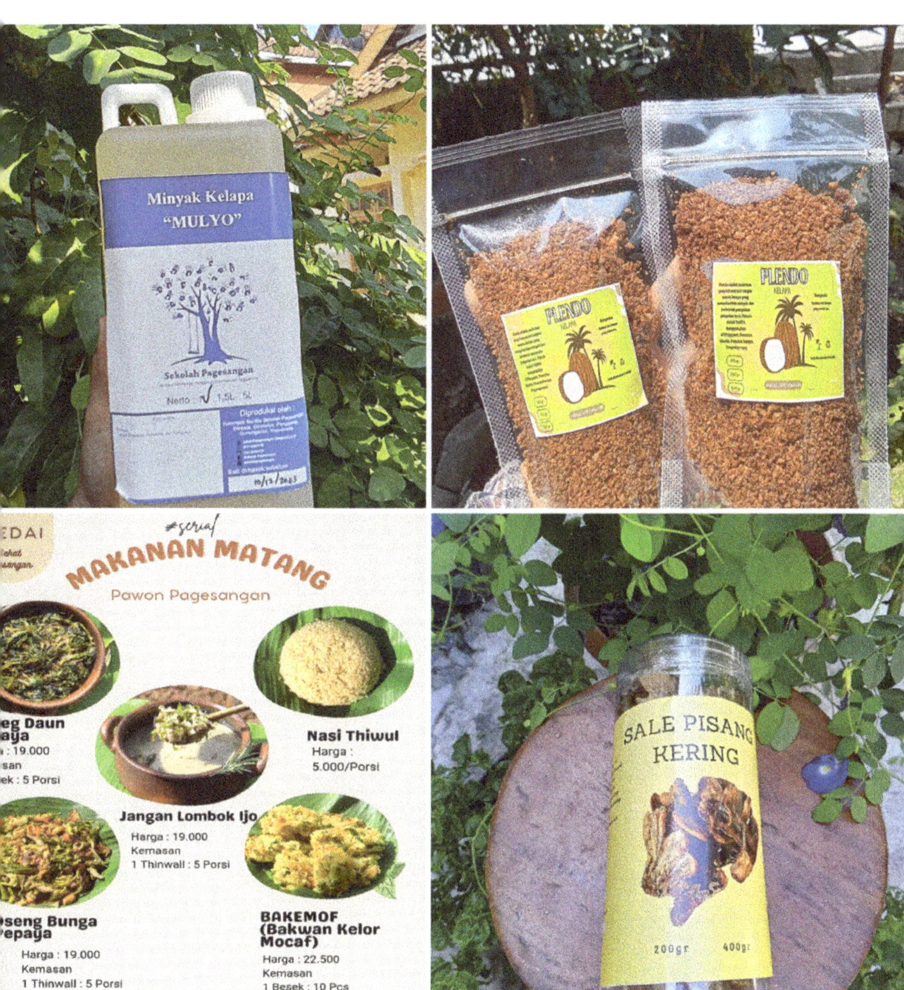

Figure 13b. Products of the Pagesangan Health Store, 2023. From left to right (top row): *minyak kelapa* (virgin coconut oil); *plendo kelapa* (coconut meal); (bottom row) various home cooked meals produced by Kedai Sehat's kitchen; *sale pisang kering* (sweet dried banana chips). Courtesy of Lifia Nuryati (Pagesangan School).

Pasucen derives from a Javanese word, *suci,* which means 'a sacred place'. It is a space to store various grains and legumes. As part of this activity, the Pagesangan members learn how to document cooking activities. The children learn how to eat various kinds of food that are no longer included in the modern family's diet. They create active connections with Gunung Kidul cultural traces.

NON-EXTRACTIVE ATTITUDE: COMMUNITY RESEARCH METHODOLOGY AND KNOWLEDGE PRODUCTION

Ethical Research, Extraction in the Field, and Precarious Knowledge

Mollo and Wintaos have become prominent research destinations for students and researchers with a variety of foci, ranging from contextual education, Indigenous knowledge, and food resilience, to textile studies and vernacular architecture.[75] Upon completion of their research projects, these researchers go back to their institutions, carrying knowledge and stories of the people. Their research outputs end up in various theses, reports, conferences, academic journals, and books. These scholarly outlets are presented as authoritative sources, but local communities do not usually have access to these academic outlets. Village and Indigenous knowledges are precarious, and face threats from various directions. In most cases, they exist as oral histories or are considered 'non-knowledge'. Their survival hinges on

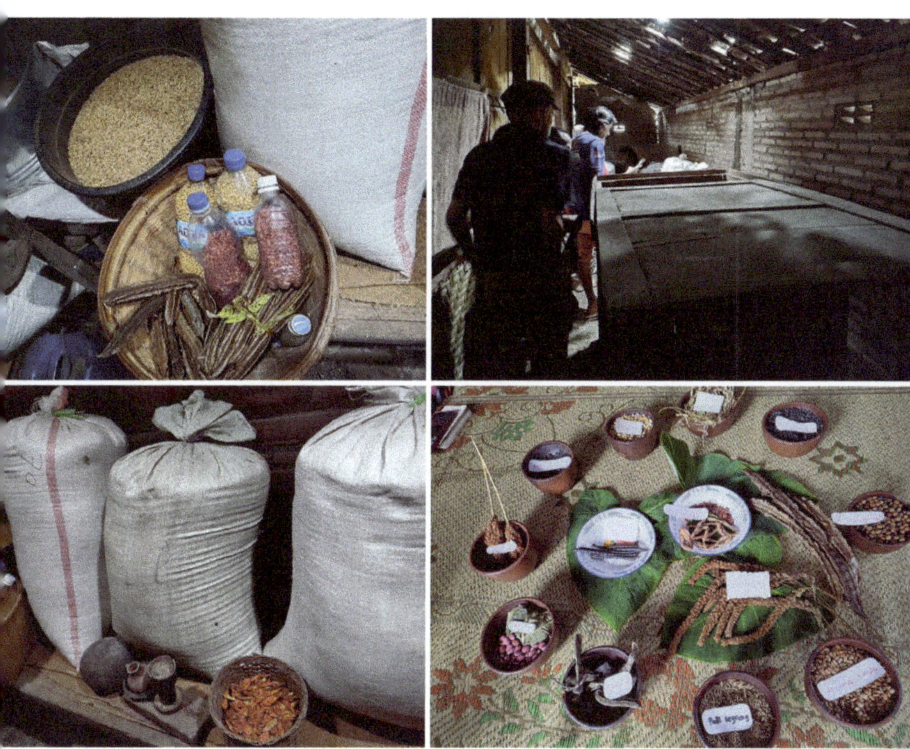

Figure 14. A visit to *Pasucen* to study the Gunung Kidul farming system, 2023. *Pasucen* is a space in which to store various grains and legumes such as *puthu* rice, *segreng* rice, black soybean, cereal, *gudhe* bean, winged bean, *tholo* bean, *benguk* bean, *koro* bean, sorghum, mung bean, and snake bean. © Nuraini Juliastuti.

the life uncertainties of elders and villagers as knowledge custodians.

To illustrate the vulnerabilities of Indigenous knowledge, I will look at two examples. First, the traffic between researchers and Lakoat.Kujawas as a community and subject of study. According to Dicky, there are long-standing imbalances whereby researchers have the power to extract local knowledge from the communities without accountable planning of how to pay them back. Dicky's statement resonates with the fate of Indigenous communities in Linda Tuhiwai Smith's research. The communities in Tuhiwai Smith's research comment that they are 'the most researched people in the world' and yet feel worthless.[76] Such worthlessness is due to the instrumentalization of Indigenous knowledge according to the politics of representation, imagination, and neoliberal drive of the research, while negating the cultural protocols and failing to address how to report back to the communities.[77] Diah's accounts of local and foreign researchers who come to Wintaos to conduct research also serve as a reminder of how taking these researchers into the village is like hosting guests.[78] There is an expectation that the Taiftob and Wintaos people should serve as good hosts who readily provide answers and explanations at the service of the researcher-guests. This often drains the hosts' time, energy, and labour, especially when such guests do not reciprocate with appreciation and reflect it in their publications.

During my research, Dicky pointed out that many European universities and museums hold valuable resources on Timorese knowledge. He continued by saying, '[we] always feel the need to go to the Netherlands because Dutch institutions have resources that the Timorese people often cannot get access to.'[79] The exclusive and restricted nature of research outlets often creates an imbalance and the feeling of being exploited. These are the feelings that are instilled into the development of an ethical foundation in Pagesangan and Lakoat.Kujawas's pedagogical practices. I connect this back to the discussion about rematriation. Such feelings resonate with Eve Tuck's critical observation about the limitation of repatriating the knowledge.[80] The return of Indonesian historical artefacts and art objects were marked by the opening exhibitions that are aptly titled *Kembali ke Tanah Merdeka* (Return to the Land of Freedom) and *Repatriasi: Kembalinya Saksi Bisu Peradaban Nusantara* (Repatriation: The Return of the Silent Witnesses of Nusantara Civilization) at the National Museum.[81] But how would this be able to return ownership of what is lost? In her research about decolonizing curriculums, Tuck emphasizes the needs to rematriate curriculum studies to make visible that the true purpose of knowledge for the Indigenous communities refers to 'the reclaiming of sovereignty, land, subsistence rights, cultural knowledge and artifacts, theories, epistemologies and axiologies'.[82]

In October 2021, members of Lakoat.Kujawas were invited to share the organization's storytelling practices in the Amsterdam Assembly for Worlding Public Cultures — an event that I helped to organize.[83] On the day of the presentation in the Assembly, Dicky posted the event on the Lakoat.Kujawas's Instagram account. This read:

> It has been almost six years that we are working together with the people of Taiftob Village, to gather our local knowledge, reproduce, and transform them into collective knowledge. Today we are invited to speak at the Amsterdam Assembly event in the Netherlands. Though this takes place only as a virtual session, this means that we have accomplished our mission. We return the local knowledge to the *kampong*, to Mollo, to Timor, the site where the knowledge was born. Youth of Mollo, we can do it. Youth of Timor, we can do it![84]

Participating in the Amsterdam Assembly was perceived as being part of the journey to return lost knowledge to its traditional owners. It might seem confusing that Dicky regarded his organization's presentation in an online event as a path to give knowledge back to the local people. I regard it as an open statement to express a sense of pride for having been acknowledged as local experts. Dicky's statement suggests that the reproduction of stories is an important element of fixing the imbalance and returning power to the people.

Second, another example of how the work of Pagesangan and Lakoat.Kujawas speaks to the vulnerabilities of Indigenous knowledge may be found in the disappearance of the *uem bubu* or *ume kbubu* (a traditional round house) from the Timorese landscape, which indicates the radically broken ties between the Mollo community and their traditional knowledge keepers (Figure 15). All parts of the house structure are inherited from ancestor knowledge to symbolize harmony. They represent the 'human relationship with nature, land, spiritual beings'.[85] In everyday life practice, an *uem bubu* functions as a 'collective food storage'.[86] I use these identifications to emphasize the infrastructural aspects of women's knowledge. *Uem bubu* serve as a means of being with the ancestral universe through ongoing recognition of the knowledge kept by women and elders. According to Lakoat.Kujawas, *uem bubu* represent not just a physical storage space, but one for collective memories and rich knowledge on Indigenous identities and biodiversity.

State development policies promote the replacement of *uem bubu* with modern houses. The policies are spurred by the idea of transforming the *uem bubu* into healthier houses. Yohannes Kambaru Windi and Andrea Whittaker's research shows that the promotion of *rumah sehat*, or healthy houses, in South Central Timor took place through the ALADIN programme in 2002.[87] Despite the depiction of *uem bubu* as unhealthy, Timorese people identify them as 'places of healing and female nurturing spaces'.[88] The unhealthy image of *uem bubu* forces Timorese communities to adopt hybridity by incorporating modified and modern features in order to maintain their traditional houses.[89] In response to this, Lakoat.Kujawas regards the disappearing *uem bubu* as the systematic 'impoverishment of the state'.[90] *Uem bubu* are stigmatized as poor. The rich knowledge and resilience attached to them is ignored. During the

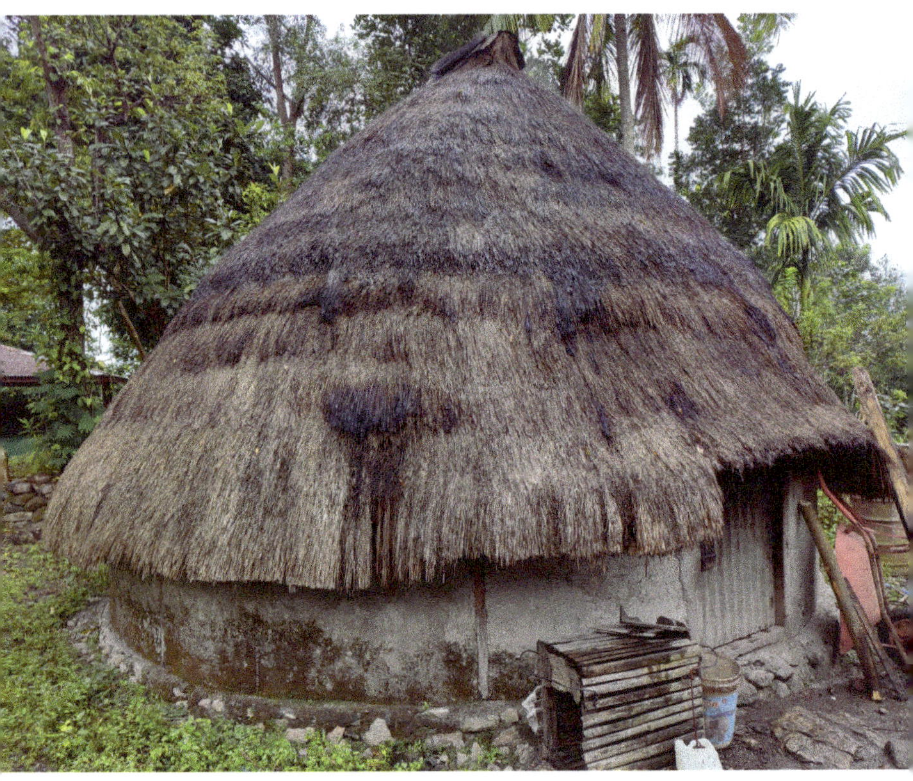

Figure 15. An *uem bubu* at the back of Bernadetta Kase, 2023. This is the housing complex of Toni Oematan, Marlinda Nau, and Bapa Fun. They are all activists from Lakoat.Kujawas, and many of the meetings took place in their houses. © Nuraini Juliastuti.

time of writing, I followed Lakoat.Kujawas's preparations to produce a work for the Biennale Jogja XVI Equator #6 Indonesia with Oceania. Their work, titled *Pah Afatis, Sonaf Aneot*, is a reconstruction of an *uem bubu*, where they installed various elements of the communities' collective memories — books, textiles, ritual items, and fermented food (Figure 16). The work signified an attempt to emphasize the infrastructural aspect of knowledge.

It might seem too obvious to connect *uem bubu* with *lumbung* (an Indonesian word for a rice barn), which was used as a curatorial concept by ruangrupa to stimulate conversation and debates around resources, economic survival, and autonomy during documenta fifteen (2022).[91] As shown throughout this iteration of documenta, using *lumbung* as a curatorial framework was intended to disrupt the usual mode of artistic performativity, which focuses on single authorship in conventional white cube aesthetics. The concept and practices of *lumbung* have since gained wider currency as tools to think about layered dimensions of resources that go beyond financial resources, and the possibilities of producing art in a different manner. This means to think about art-making while at the same time thinking about principles about how to live and behave in relation to the well-being of the collective ecosystem. I retain *uem bubu* as well as *pasucen* and local collective pots within the contexts of Mollo and Wintaos as a way to respect the complexity of their vernacular meanings, while acknowledging their resonance with similar practices in various Global South contexts. I perceive this as a way to minimize the risk

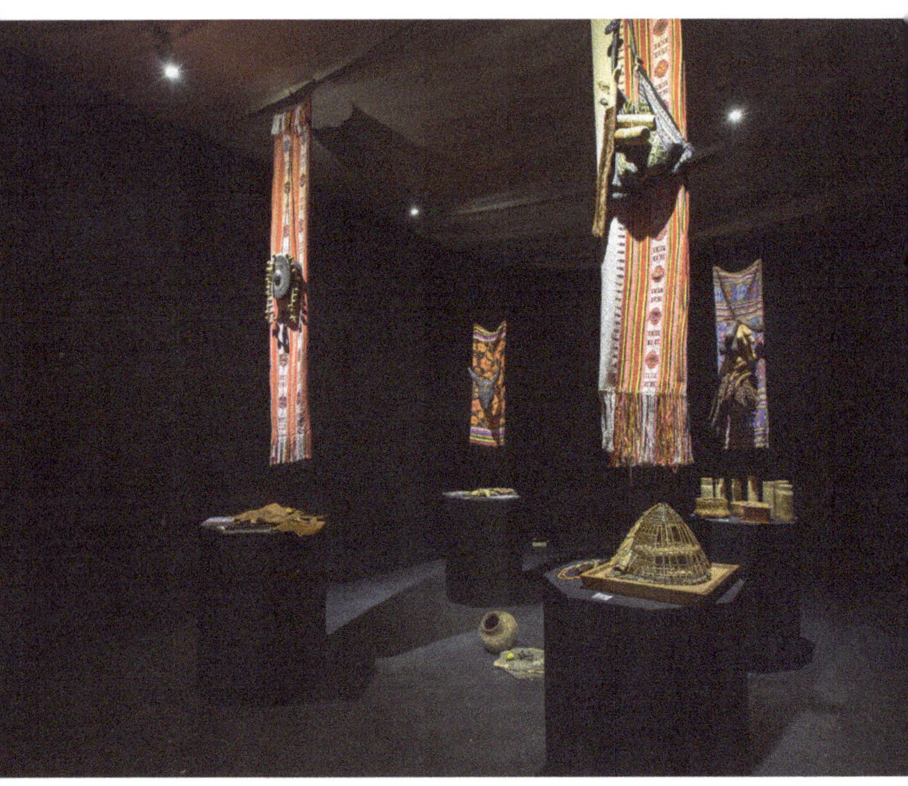

Figure 16. *Pah Afatis, Sonaf Aneot*, 2021. Courtesy of Biennale Jogja.

of *uem bubu* or *pasucen* being reduced to a representational object and translation of collective and collaborative practices within transnational contemporary art settings.

Contextual Education: On Jet Lag and a Pedagogy Model that Teaches Us to Stay

Among the community members in Wintaos, Pagesangan is often dubbed *sekolah bukan-bukan*, or the 'impossible school'. Pagesangan does not want to be trapped into evaluation standards and measurement systems set up by formal institutions. The contextual principles of Pagesangan lie in its agility to grapple with various dead ends in everyday problems. It works to ensure sustainability — a long-lasting chain of wisdom. For the youth of Wintaos, obtaining education promises a certain kind of vertical mobility. Everyday life always demands immediate action. Making an early start in the workforce is considered desirable, as this provides income to fulfil a family's everyday needs. There have been some lingering feelings that conventional schooling would not equip students with the tools they need to deal with everyday problems.

In the words of Diah, school engenders 'jet lag'. In this context, jet lag refers to tiredness resulting from a disconnection between what to absorb from school, what to expect from being at school, and what one experiences on a daily basis. Diah refers to the science obtained from formal education institutions as *ilmu pergi*, literally the science of leaving. In practice, Wintaos people also need to go outside their village in order to go to school. Education infrastructures are not part of the village-scapes. Rather than rootedness, the science of leaving teaches people to be alienated from their ancestral social environments. Their existence disregards other ways of knowing and visions which have existed as part of the community's survival system. Pagesangan School's contextual learning system is propelled by a vision to reconnect with the village's knowledge histories.

Method of Knowledge Production: Studying, Archiving, and Surviving as Areas for Tooling

In this section, I tie together various non-extractive attitudes discussed in the previous section. These include the reproduction of stories, a desire to develop an infrastructure for salient matters which would be otherwise homeless, and the idea of home as the basis of knowledge to reorient the directions of what to study and gather. One of the most important functions of Pagesangan and Lakoat.Kujawas is their operation of alternative schools — the Pagesangan School and Skol Tomolok, respectively. These schools operationalize non-extractive attitudes, which later serve as the basis for developing a method of knowledge production. This puts practical, locally usable education at the heart of the workings of a museum.

In the diagram depicted in Figure 17, I show how the methodology of knowledge production in the commons museum works. Pagesangan School and Skol Tomolok serve as contextual educational laboratories. As schools, they are empowered by studying, archiving, and surviving. These three modes of working are intertwined and overlap with one another. They emerge as sites where modes of survival also become the foci of joint study. Moments of archiving turn into studying, which later become paths for surviving. These paths for surviving lead to practices of archiving and studying everyday life. The entanglement of studying, archiving, and surviving addresses various questions around access, extraction, autonomy, and sovereignty. They support the operationalization of the pillars of both organizations through vernacular archiving, radical pedagogies, and community economies. This process produces a collection of archives and knowledge that signifies the constant effort to deal with different urgencies.

CONCLUDING NOTES

I began this research with the intention of theorizing the archival production emerging from Pagesangan and Lakoat.Kujawas' pedagogical practices. Seeing these organizations as commons museums troubled existing definitions of the museum and education institutions that have been taken for granted. At the same time, it also emphasizes the potential capaciousness of the formal museum and education institutions. The conceptualization of commons museums has allowed me to explore community restoration projects in two main ways. First, in terms of the perpetuation of village knowledge, and, second, by highlighting

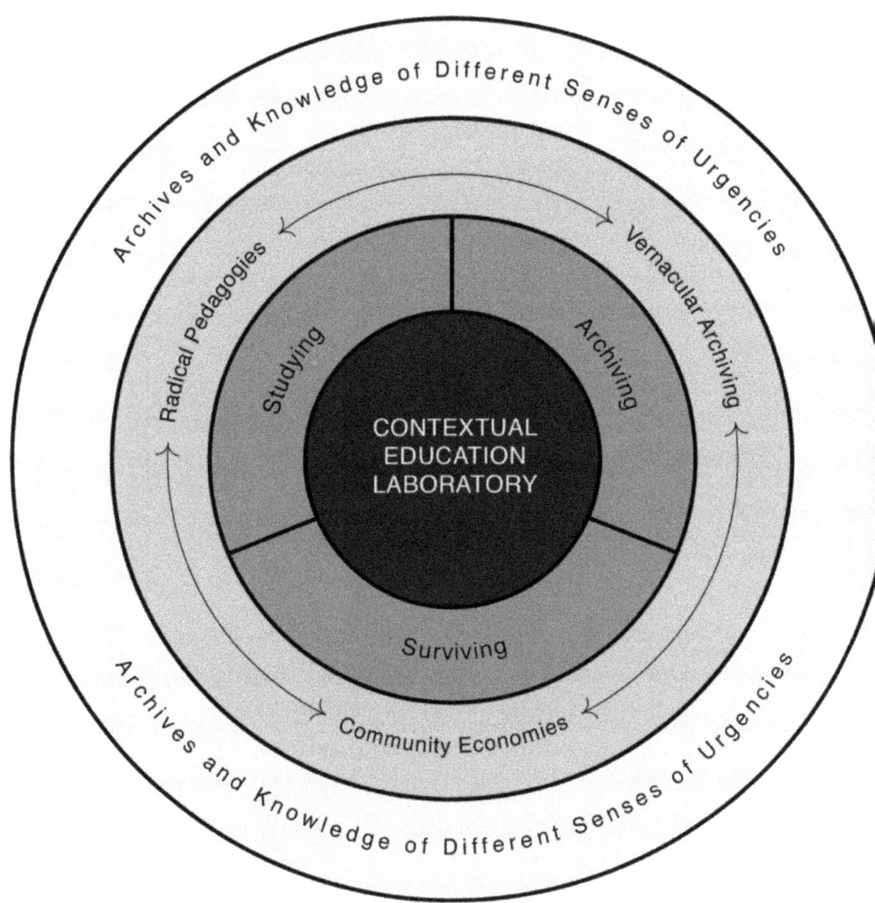

Figure 17. Commons Museums: Method of Knowledge Production.
© Nuraini Juliastuti.

the development of community research projects that are more ethical and directed towards the development of various working areas where Pagesangan and Lakoat.Kujawas revitalize traditions and bring collective awareness of various disappearing knowledges. They include creating a new generation of storytellers who are able to move back and forth between intergenerational stories and justice, and developing a resilient community support system through identifying the richness of the social ecosystem by preserving local foods and generating new learners of vernacular farming systems.

The meaning of heritage, and the question of what may be inherited, relies on an understanding of the self in relation to overcoming the feeling of being extracted and reproducing precarious knowledge. The principle that governs material accumulation in commons museums is not geared towards collecting objects. Rather, it is orientated towards transforming different senses of urgency into collective archives. Pagesangan and Lakoat.Kujawas provide spaces for developing methods for studying together. Pedagogy serves as a means to return and take ownership of things that have been lost. Commons museums, therefore, also invite a reimagining of public institutions from informal and collective practices. They serve as creative platforms where the community identifies and tackles their existing problems, create strategies of resistance to neoliberal ideas of progress, and think of alternative scenarios to deal with them. This shows an attempt to remake their lives, devising a more conducive and workable living arrangement. The timeline of commons museums is based on what these organizations feel the urge to show, explore, and connect with. To think through 'what is left' allows a further observation of how the processes of remaking life are based less on looking ahead and more on looking at the past, unearthing forgotten and abandoned knowledges, and filling in the meanings of various matters that have been emptied. The workings of commons museums centre around everything that produces life; Pagesangan and Lakoat.Kujawas perform the logics of post-authoritarian archiving and commoning in a time of crisis.

NOTES

1 Donna J. Haraway, *Staying with the Trouble: Making Kin in the Chthlucene* (Durham, NC: Duke University Press, 2016).

2 Ibid., p. 76.

3 See the final report of the museum definition. The document can be accessed here: <https://icom.museum/wp-content/uploads/2022/07/EN_EGA2022_MuseumDefinition_WDoc_Final-2.pdf> [accessed 20 November 2023]. For more information about the multiple stages of the consultation process, which led to the decision, see, 'Museum Definition', *International Council of Museums* <https://icom.museum/en/resources/standards-guidelines/museum-definition/> [accessed 27 February 2024].

4 L'Internationale confederation comprises sixteen institutions: Museo Reina Sofia (Spain), MACBA (Spain), M HKA (Belgium), MSN (Poland), Salt (Turkey), Van Abbemuseum (the Netherlands), MSU (Croatia), Haus der Kulturen der Welt (Germany), HDK-Valand (Sweden), NCAD (Ireland), ZRC SAZU (Slovenia), Institute for Radical Imagination (Italy), Tranzit.ro (Romania), Visual Culture Research Center (Ukraine), IMMA (Ireland), WIELS (Belgium), and L'Internationale Association. The project description cited above was taken from Van Abbemuseum's website. See, 'L'Internationale', *Van Abbemuseum*, <https://vanabbemuseum.nl/en/museum/support-the-museum/linternationale> [accessed 27 February 2024].

5 There has been public demand for the return of Indonesian artefacts, alongside the popularization of the concept around *koloniale roofkunst* — stolen artworks from the colony, combined with an awareness of the need to protect national heritage. One of the culminating points was the restitution of 1500 Indonesian artefacts and art objects to Indonesia in 2020, which had been held in the Museum Nusantara (and later in Museum Prinsenhof) in Delft, the Netherlands.

Meanwhile, the National Museum of World Cultures/Nationaal Museum van Wereldculturen (NMVW) in the Netherlands is leading the public discourse around decolonization and the possibility of creating museums as caring spaces. The Research Center of Material Culture (RCMC), the research flagship of the NMVW, led the PPROCE, Provenance Research on Objects of the Colonial Era. To learn more about the project and to download the reports, see, 'PPROCE — Provenance Research on Objects of the Colonial Era', *Wereldmuseum Leiden* <https://www.volkenkunde.nl/en/our-collection/pproce-provenance-research-on-objects-colonial-era> [accessed 20 November 2023]. There are also new initiatives to situate the questions of restitution at the intersection of research and art practices, social reconciliation, and provenance. *Pressing Matter*, which was organized by Vrije Universiteit and Research Center of Material Culture is a case in point. To learn more about the project, see, 'Pressing Matter: Ownership, Value and the Question of Colonial Heritage in Museums', *Pressing Matter* <https://pressingmatter.nl/> [accessed 27 February 2024].

6   Paul Basu, 'Object Diasporas, Resourcing Communities: Sierra Leonean Collections in the Global Museumscape', *Museum Anthropology*, 34.1 (2011), pp. 28–42 (p. 37).

7   Ibid.

8   See Laura Peers and Allison K. Brown, 'Introduction', in *Museum and Source Communities: A Routledge Reader*, ed. by Laura Peers and Allison K. Brown (London: Routledge, 2003), pp. 1–17 (p. 2).

9   Clare Harris, 'Digital Dilemmas: The Ethnographic Museum as Distributive Institution', *Journal of the Anthropological Society of Oxford*, 5.2 (2013), pp. 125–36 (pp. 125–27).

10   Nishi Doshi, 'Calling for "Rematriation": Art, Heritage, and Sovereignty', in *Climate Justice Code for Artists, Art Workers and Art Organisations Situated in the Global North*, ed. by Climate Justice Code Working Group (Utrecht: Casco Art Institute: Working for the Commons, 2023), pp. 83–92 (p. 86).

11   Ibid.

12   James Clifford, 'Museums as Contact Zones', in *Routes: Travel and Translation in the Late Twentieth Century*, ed. by James Clifford (Cambridge, MA: Harvard University Press, 1997), pp. 188–219 (p. 213).

13   Ruth B. Phillips, 'Re-Placing Objects: Historical Practices for the Second Museum Age', *Canadian Historical Review*, 86.1 (2005), pp. 83–110.

14   Ruth B. Phillips, 'Introduction: Community Collaborations in Exhibitions: Toward a Dialogic Paradigm', in *Museum and Source Communities*, ed. by Laura Peers and Alison K. Brown, pp. 155–70 (p. 158).

15   Robin Boast, 'Neocolonial Collaboration: Museum as Contact Zone Revisited', *Museum Anthropology*, 34.1 (2011), pp. 56–70.

16   Ibid., p. 66.

17   Charlotte Hess and Elinor Ostrom, 'Introduction: An Overview of the Knowledge Commons', in *Understanding Knowledge as Commons: From Theory to Practice*, ed. by Charlotte Hess and Elinor Ostrom (Cambridge, MA: The MIT Press, 2006), pp. 3–26 (p. 8).

18   See Eko Haryono, Didit Hadi Barianto, and Ahmad Cahyadi, 'Petunjuk Kegiatan Lapangan: Hidrogeologi Kawasan Karst Gunung Sewu' [Field Guide: Hydrogeology of Gunung Sewu Karst Region], in *Pekan Ilmiah Tahunan Perhimpunan Ahli Airtanah Indonesia* [Annual Science Week of the Association of Indonesian Groundwater Specialists], *INA-Rxiv*, 14 September 2017, pp. 1–33 (p. 1) <https://doi.org/10.31227/osf.io/t5dgp>.

19   See the Poverty Alleviation plan of 2021 provided by the Regional Body for Planning and Development, Special Region of Yogyakarta Province. Based on this data, the definition of people who live below the poverty line referred to those who had earned income under 482,855 IDR per month (approximately 29 EUR). See, 'Pengentasan Kemiskinan' [Poverty Alleviation], *Bappeda DIY* [Provincial Development Planning Agency, Special Region of Yogyakarta] <http://bappeda.jogjaprov.go.id/dataku/infografik/kemiskinan> [accessed 5 February 2022].

20   Dharmaningtyas, *Pulung Gantung: Menyingkap Tragedi Bunuh Diri di Gunungkidul* [Pulung Gantung: Revealing Suicide Tragedies in Gunungkidul] (Yogyakarta: Salwa Press, 2002). On the same subject, see also

Iman Budhi Santosa and Wage Daksinarga, *Tali Pati: Kisah-kisah Bunuh Diri di Gunung Kidul* [Rope of Death: Stories of Suicide in Gunung Kidul] (Yogyakarta: Jalasutra, 2003). Within local cosmology, *pulung gantung* also refers to a celestial object that appears to signal the suicides. This link seems to dodge the discussion around poverty. Unfortunately, this important topic is beyond the scope of this chapbook.

21 *Gaber* refers to the waste of tapioca flour or 'dried oilcake'. *Gaber* is also a Javanese word for the act of vomiting and spitting out food that has been chewed. During this period, people were forced to eat the leaves and insides of stems from various plants that were often inedible.

22 Diah Widuretno, 'Belajar dari Gaber, Atasi Ancaman Krisis Pangan Pandemi Corona' [Learning from *gaber* in Dealing with Food Crisis amidst Corona Pandemic], *Historead*, 25 June 2021 <https://web.archive.org/web/20210921074950/https://historead.co.id/belajar-dari-gaber-atasi-ancaman-krisis-pangan-pandemi-corona/> [accessed 2 February 2022].

23 Yunita Khusnul Khotimah, Suprapti Supardi, and Ernoiz Antriyandarti, 'Pemanfaatan Sumber Daya Pertanian Lahan Kering di Pegunungan Karst Gunung Kidul' [The Utilization of Agricultural Resources in the Drylands in the Gunung Kidul Karst Mountain], in *Seminar Nasional Sumber Daya Pertanian Berkelanjutan dalam Mendukung Ketahanan dan Keamanan Pangan Indonesia pada Era Revolusi Industri 4.0* [Sustainable Agricultural Resources in Supporting Food Resiliency and Security in Indonesia during Industrial Revolution Era 4.0], *Prosiding Seminar Nasional Fakultas Pertanian*, 3.1 (2019), pp. 50–57.

24 Diah Widuretno, 'Belajar Mengamankan Pangan dari Masyarakat Wintaos, Gunungkidul' [Learning to Secure Food from Wintaos, Gunungkidul], *Mojok*, 11 May 2023 <https://mojok.co/podium/belajar-mengamankan-pangan-dari-masyarakat-wintaos-gunungkidul/> [accessed 11 May 2023].

25 Sahid Susanto, 'Mengingat Jaman Gaber' [Remembering Jaman Gaber], *Cerita Fakta Sumberdaya Alam Tropis*, 16 December 2015 <https://ceritafaktasumberdayaalamtropis.tp.ugm.ac.id/index.php/cerita-fakta/cerita-fakta-alam-liar-6/5-mengingat-jaman-gaber> [accessed 12 July 2022].

26 Diah Widuretno, 'Benih, Pangan dan Kehidupan' [Seeds, Food, and Life], *Historead*, 1 August 2021 <https://web.archive.org/web/20210921172859/https://historead.co.id/benih-pangan-dan-kehidupan/> [accessed 4 February 2022]

27 The New Order refers to the authoritarian presidency of Soeharto (from 1967 to 1998). Corruption, collusion, and nepotism were emblematic of the Soeharto regime (which was backed by the military). During the New Order era, various tensions and conflicts emerged from the oppression of human rights, freedom of expression, different initiatives, and the burgeoning of ideas.

28 See Anna L. Tsing, *Friction: An Ethnography of Global Connection* (Princeton, NJ: Princeton University Press, 2005), p. 153.

29 See *Sumber Sejarah Lisan Revolusi Hijau di Indonesia* (Sources of Oral Histories: The Green Revolution in Indonesia), ed. by Mona Lohanda (Jakarta: Kementrian Pendidikan dan Kebudayaan Republik Indonesia, 2017), p. 71. *Pancasila* is the Sanskrit word meaning Five Principles, the official philosophical foundation of Indonesia.

30 Diah Widuretno, 'Seeds, Food, and Life'.

31 Diah Widuretno, *Gesang di Lahan Gersang* [Life in the Barren Land] (Yogyakarta: CV Putra Surya Santosa and Sekolah Pagesangan, 2020).

32 To learn more about mining in Timor, see 'Marble Mining in Indigenous Mollo Territory in West Timor, Indonesia', *Ej Atlas*, last updated 14 October 2021 <https://ejatlas.org/conflict/marble-mining-in-indigenous-mollo-territory-in-west-timor-indonesia> [accessed 2 October 2022], and the report 'Hungry Coal: Coal Mining and Food Security in Indonesia', *JATAM*, 8 May 2017 <https://www.jatam.org/en/hungry-coal-coal-mining-and-food-security-in-indonesia/> [accessed 2 October 2022].

33 Febriana Firdaus, 'The Battle of the Mountains of Mollo', *The Gecko Project*, 20 November 2020 <https://thegeckoproject.org/articles/the-battle-for-the-mountains-of-mollo/> [accessed 20 March 2021]. This article is part of a series about women, rural communities, and resistance to corporations and ecological destruction. The film, *Our Mothers' Land*, directed by Leo Plunkett (The Gecko Project and Mongabay, 2020) emerged from the series. The film is available on YouTube, 2 No-

vember 2020 <https://www.youtube.com/watch?v=xwro9TsU2mE> [accessed 23 March 2021].

34 This is based on the Study of Indonesian Nutrition Status on National, Provinces, Municipalities, and Cities Level 2021, issued by the Ministry of Health, 27 December 2021. To compare, the Provincial Snapshot: East Nusa Tenggara, Sustainable Development Goals for Children in Indonesia, states that the province has a 43 per cent rate of stunted children in 2020.

35 The data from the Indonesian Migrant Workers Union states that from 2011 to 2018, 243 migrant workers from East Nusa Tenggara province died. See '6 Tahun Setelah Ratifikasi Konvensi Migran, Kasus Kematian BMI NTT Meningkat' [Six Years After Ratification of the International Convention on the Protection of the Rights of All Migrant Workers and Members of Their Families, The Death Cases of Migrant Workers from East Nusa Tenggara is Rising], *SBMI* [Indonesian Migrant Workers Union], 26 March 2018 <https://sbmi.or.id/6-tahun-setelah-ratifikasi-konvensi-migran-kasus-kematian-bmi-ntt-meningkat/> [accessed 2 February 2022]. A local online news portal, *Floresku*, reported that between 2018 and 2021, deceased migrant workers numbered 409 people. See, 'Aduh, 409 Pekerja Migran NTT Gugur di Luar Negeri Dalam Kurun Kurang dari 4 Tahun' [409 Migrant Workers from East Nusa Tenggara Died in Less Than Four Years], *Floresku*, 11 October 2021 <https://floresku.com/read/aduh-409-pekerja-migran-ntt-gugur-di-luar-negeri-dalam-kurun-kurang-dari-4-tahun> [accessed 2 February 2022].

36 Tania Murray Li, *Land's End: Capitalist Relations on an Indigenous Frontier* (Durham, NC: Duke University Press, 2014), p. 8.

37 This reflection about the village emerged during an interview between Diah Widuretno and Kalis Mardiasih (Pares Indonesia). The title of the interview is *A Free School without Uniform in the Village*. See, 'Membuat Sekolah di Desa tanpa Seragam dan Bayar SPP | Diah Widuretno (Sekolah Pagesangan)', YouTube, 4 February 2022, <https://www.youtube.com/watch?v=iAdJPaQuKCY&t=35s> [accessed 5 February 2022].

38 When the financial crisis hit Southeast Asia, it combined with the on-going struggles against human rights abuses and suppression of creative freedom during the New Order regime, which led to the waves of student protests across Indonesian cities as well as military violence. It culminated in the resignation of Soeharto on 21 May 1998. The period of transition that began with the fall of Soeharto is known as the Post-Reformation era (*Reformasi*) or Post-Soeharto era. *Reformasi* has given rise to increased activity in new cultural production, which was fuelled by an urgency to manifest a long-suppressed counter-culture movement.

39 The popularity of hashtags such as #mositidakpercaya (a no-trust motion), #reformasidikorupsi (reformation has been corrupted), #pandemidibajakoligarki (the pandemic has been hijacked by the oligarchy), and most recently #impeachjokowi (impeach Jokowi) — the popular name of President Joko Widodo — demonstrates growing dissatisfaction with the state. Another popular hashtag at the time of the writing is #percumalaporpolisi, which means 'reporting to the police is useless'. There is a desperate tone in the sentence. Waiting for the authorities to take action only means suffering from injustice for longer. People acknowledge the need to take matters into their own hands.

40 In this chapbook, I have portrayed the Indigenous and rural communities' shared struggles to retain their lands and keep their cultures alive. But the case of Indigenous communities in Indonesia is more complicated. Monica Ndoen's report in the Indonesia Country Report Section of the 37th edition of the Indigenous World 2023, pp. 207–13, states that at the official level, Indonesia rejects the concept of Indigenous People in the United Nations Declarations on the Rights of Indigenous Peoples (UNDRIP). The basis of the argument is that a large part of the Indonesian population, all but the ethnic Chinese, is considered Indigenous. However, there has been a rise in the annexation of Indigenous territories to promote certain elements of the state agenda. These include the expansion of social forestry programmes (which expel the Indigenous people from their own lands), an increase in national infrastructure projects (which has intensified through the passing of the Job Creation Omnibus Law in 2020 and further destroys land for neoliberal purposes), and the diminishing rights of the Indigenous people

to govern their land. See also the Indigenous People's Alliance of the Archipelago's report, which shows that the new bill on Criminal Code 2022 bears the potential to violate and criminalize Indigenous peoples. See, 'Pengaturan "Hukum yang Hidup" dalam RKUHP, Melanggar Hak Masyarakat Adat' [Regulation of the Living Law in the Criminal Code Bill, violates the rights of the Indigenous Peoples], *AMAN*, 2 December 2022 <https://www.aman.or.id/news/read/1507> [accessed 25 November 2023].

41 In February 2022, Samin community members in Wadas Village, Central Java, met with atrocities when military forces used violence to suppress their protests against andesite mining. See GEMPADEWA's Instagram account @wadas_melawan. The residents of Sangihe Island Regency, North Sulawesi, have been in ongoing negotiations and constant protests against gold mining in the area (see Save Sangihe Island's Instagram account @save.sangihe). Social media plays a role in conveying messages to the wider public. Both accounts have been active since 2018, and they maintain their presence by updating the public with recent news related to the issues. Observation on these Instagram accounts will make clear that direct confrontation with the military is always an expected occurrence through the duration of their struggles.

42 The popularity of #wargabantuwarga (citizens helping citizens) and #salingjaga (taking care of each other) hashtags in social media indicates this.

43 Doreen Lee, *Activist Archives: Youth Culture and the Political Past in Indonesia* (Durham, NC: Duke University Press, 2016), p. 213.

44 Sekolah Salah Didik (School of Improper Education) is a long-term project organized by Yogyakarta-based Kunci Study Forum & Collective. Established in 2020, Sekolah Pemikiran Perempuan (The School of Women's Thought) is 'an initiative that intervenes in the processes of knowledge production that marginalize, invalidate and erase women'. In 2018, Sekolah Budaya Mbrosot (Mbrosot Cultural School) was born. Hersri Setiawan and Ita Fatia Nadia initiated the school. Mbrosot's pedagogical concept is rooted in the activism of Setiawan and Nadia — feminism, human rights, and cultural movement. Another strand of school-based activities is situated in the intersection of art and edu-

cation. Gudskul is a shared space, designed to pool their intellectual and creative resources. Three Jakarta-based collectives — ruangrupa, Serrum, and Grafis Huru Hara — occupy the space. The existence of Gudskul can be contextualized within critiques of conventional art education institutions. The following websites explore examples in more detail: Kunci Study Forum & Collective <http://kunci.or.id/>, School of Improper Education <http://sekolah.kunci.or.id>, Sekolah Pemikiran Perempuan <http://pemikiranperempuan.org/>, Gudskul <http://gudskul.art/> [all accessed on 16 June 2022].

45 Nuraini Juliastuti, *Commons People: Managing Music and Culture in Contemporary Yogyakarta* (unpublished doctoral thesis, Leiden University, 2019), p. 23.

46 See Stefano Harney and Fred Moten, 'Debt and Study' in *The Undercommons: Fugitive Planning and Black Study* (Wivenhoe, New York: Minor Compositions, 2013), pp. 61–68.

47 Ibid., p. 20.

48 Based on my experience, developing clandestine study groups became part of the student movement's strategic plans to sow critical thought during the New Order regime in the 1990s.

49 For critical analysis of Taman Siswa, see Kenji Tsuchiya, 'The Taman Siswa Movement — Its Early Eight Years and Javanese Background', *Journal of Southeast Asian Studies*, 6.2 (1975), pp. 164–77, and also Kenji Tsuchiya and Peter Hawkes, *Democracy and Leadership: The Rise of the Taman Siswa Movement in Indonesia* (Honolulu: University of Hawai'i Press, 1987).

50 See Hilmar Farid and Razif, 'Batjaan Liar in the Dutch East Indies: A Colonial Antipode', *Postcolonial Studies*, 11.3 (2008), pp. 277–92.

51 See Nuraini Juliastuti, 'Sanggar as a Model for Practicing Art in Communal Life', in *Made in Commons Monograph*, ed. by Ferdiansyah Thajib and Kerstin Winking (Amsterdam: Stedelijk Museum Bureau Amsterdam; Yogyakarta: KUNCI Cultural Studies Center, 2013), pp. 9–17.

52 In a different context, the meaning of *sanggar* can also be connected with the Bramacharya Ashram initiated by Rabindranath Tagore. According to Sanchayan Ghosh, in the 'ashrama education', Tagore explores

pedagogy as 'an interface for transforming the relationship between the individual and the collective in the context of a specific location' (see Sanchayan Ghosh, 'Circl(e)ing Inside Out: Tools for Pedagogy as Art Practice', *March: Journal of Art and Strategy Special Volume: Tools for Radical Study* (2024), ed. by KUNCI Study Forum & Collective, pp. 28–63.

53   For example, see Museum Biologi (Biology Museum), an educational museum established by the Faculty of Biology, Gadjah Mada University, Yogyakarta, in 1969. See also Museum Karst Indonesia in Wonogiri Municipality, Central Java. The operationalization of the museum is effected through the Faculty of Engineering, Gadjah Mada University.

54   The Sultanate of Yogyakarta (Keraton Ngayogyakarta Hadiningrat) organizes four museums in the palace (*keraton*). They are Museum Lukisan (Painting Museum), Museum Sri Sultan Hamengkubuwono IX, Museum Kereta (Royal Carriage Museum), and Museum Batik. There is also Museum Sonobudoyo, managed by the Regional Technical Implementation Unit, Yogyakarta Special Region Cultural Office. In Kupang, there is Museum Daerah Nusa Tenggara Timur (Regional Museum of East Nusa Tenggara), which was established in 1977 and is now managed by the Education and Culture Unit, East Nusa Tenggara Province.

55   There are three museums in Yogyakarta that focus on the colonial war and struggle for independence. They are the Fort Vredeburg Museum, Monumen Jogja Kembali (Return of Jogja Monument), and Museum Perjuangan (Museum of Struggles). Vredeburg displays various dioramas and artefacts that depict independence struggles during Dutch occupation. Monument Jogja Kembali was established to commemorate the crucial period from 1945 to 1949 during the armed conflict and diplomatic resistance to Dutch military aggression against the Indonesian proclamation of independence on 17 August 1945. Museum Perjuangan is a post-war museum. It was established to commemorate the National Awakening Day, which takes place every year on 20 May. It is interesting to note here that Yogyakarta has more museums designed from a militaristic-heroic perspective than East Nusa Tenggara province. The need to emphasize the important role of Yogyakarta as the centre of the struggle during the colonial wars is always strong.

56 Museum H. M. Soeharto is a memorial dedicated to the life of Soeharto. The museum depicts Soeharto's early life, military career, and national and international achievements during his presidency and his life following his resignation in 1998. By celebrating his life, the museum sustains the official narratives of Indonesia from a New Order perspective.

57 Benedict Anderson, *Imagined Communities: Reflections on the Origin and Spread of Nationalism* (London: Verso, 2006), p. 183.

58 Pramoedya Ananta Toer, *Rumah Kaca* [House of Glass] (Jakarta: Lentera Dipantara, 2010).

59 Museum HAM Munir is 'a civilization museum' dedicated to commemorating the life of Munir Said Thalib, the Indonesian human rights and anti-corruption activist who was assassinated due to his activism. Medayu Agung is a library and reading room built by Oei Hiem Hwie, a former political prisoner, to collect a variety of reading material, which survived political violence in the post-colonial and New Order regimes. @1965setiaphari (Everyday 1965) is a moving museum dedicated to preserving communist archives and memories of the families of political prisoners and Indonesian Communist Party members. @discoverlasem, a heritage and guided tour dedicated to listing Indo-Chinese heritage sites. Pusara Digital is a digital museum to remind us of the death of people and health workers during the pandemic, a story of state neglect. Ruang Arsip & Sejarah Perempuan (A Room for Archives and Histories of Women) is an educational research centre to document stories and histories of forgotten women. Kunci Study Forum & Collective is a research base, which I co-founded in 1999, and which also started its practices by organizing family and kampong history projects.

60 Rudolf Mrazek, *Engineers of Happy Land: Technology and Nationalism in a Colony* (Princeton, NJ: Princeton University Press, 2002), p. xvii.

61 Joshua Barker, and others, 'Figures of Indonesian Modernity', *Indonesia*, 87 (2009), pp. 35–72 (p. 38).

62 Arturo Escobar, *Designs for the Pluriverse: Radical Interdependence, Autonomy, and the Making of Worlds* (Durham, NC: Duke University Press, 2018).

63 Humberto Maturana and Francisco Varela, *Autopoiesis and Cognition: The Realization of the Living* (Boston, MA: Reidel, 1980), p. 79.

64 Escobar, *Designs for the Pluriverse*, p. 172.

65 Ibid., pp. 5–6.

66 On the British Council's website, Dicky is represented as an exemplary active citizen. The description of British Council Active Citizens was derived from the British Council's organization website. See, 'Social Innovation in South East Asia Programme, Case Studies Series: Active Citizens in Universities and Communities', *British Council*, April 2021 <https://www.britishcouncil.org/sites/default/files/sharing_values_and_visions_for_social_change_sisea_case_study_4.pdf> [accessed 24 March 2022].

67 Katherine McKittrick, *Dear Science and Other Stories* (Durham, NC: Duke University Press, 2021), p. 7.

68 Ibid.

69 See Resi Nati, and others, *Surat-surat dari Mollo: Sekumpulan Resep dan Cerita* [Letters from Mollo: An Anthology of Recipes and Stories] (Mollo: Lakoat.Kujawas, 2023).

70 *Mustika Rasa: Resep Masakan Indonesia Warisan Sukarno* (*Mustika Rasa: Indonesian Cuisine Recipes and Sukarno's Heritage*), ed. by JJ Rizal (Jakarta: Komunitas Bambu, 2016).

71 Ibid., p. iv.

72 Amiruddin Al Rahab, *Ekonomi Berdikari Sukarno* [Sukarno's Berdikari Economy] (Jakarta: Komunitas Bambu, 2014).

73 Tsing, *Friction*, p. 156.

74 See also Gatari Suryakusuma, 'Pagesangan School: Preserving Food Knowledge in Wintaos Village, Panggang', *Gunung Kidul, Jurnal Bakudapan*, 2 (2019), pp. 78–98.

75 The work of Gerry van Klinken, *The Making of Middle Indonesia: Middle Classes in Kupang Towns 1930s–1980s* (Leiden: Brill, 2014) serves as an important reference for many community organizers in East Nusa Tenggara, including Dicky.

76 Linda Tuhiwai Smith, *Decolonizing Methodologies: Research and Indigenous Peoples* (London: Zed Books; Dunedin: University of Otago Press, 1999), pp. 8–9.

77 Ibid., pp. 14–17.

78 Personal conversation with Diah Widuretno in May 2023. The subject of how visits from researchers, schools, universities, and community organizers affected the villagers' perspective on their roles as knowledge-keepers kept on resurfacing during our many conversations since this research started in December 2020.

79 Personal conversation with Dicky Senda in December 2022. A further conversation about this took place during my recent visit to Mollo in summer 2023.

80 Eve Tuck, 'Rematriating Curriculum Studies', *Journal of Curriculum and Pedagogy*, 8.1 (2011), pp. 34–37.

81 The exhibition *Kembali ke Tanah Merdeka* (Return to the Land of Freedom) commemorated the return of artefacts and art objects from Museum Nusantara (Delft) from 12 December 2020 to 11 January 2021 at the National Museum of Indonesia. The exhibition *Repatriasi: Kembalinya Saksi Bisu Peradaban Nusantara* (Repatriation: The Return of the Silent Witnesses of Nusantara Civilization) commemorated the return of artefacts and art objects objects from the Wereldmuseum Leiden (previously Museum Volkenkunde) from 28 November to 10 December 2023.

82 Tuck, 'Rematriating Curriculum Studies', p. 35.

83 'Amsterdam Assembly: Letting Go of Having to Speak All the Time' was a gathering and thinking space for activists, artists, scholars, and other cultural practitioners to discuss various topics around decolonization, pedagogy, racism, and the politics of archiving. It was organized by Vrije Universiteit Amsterdam, University of Amsterdam, and the Research Center for Material Culture at Framer Framed, from 7 to 9 October 2021. The event was part of the 'Worlding Public Culture: The Arts and Social Innovation' project. To learn more about the programme, see 'Amsterdam Assembly: Letting Go of Having to Speak All the Time', *Framer Framed*, <https://framerframed.nl/en/projecten/amsterdam-assembly/> and 'Amsterdam Assembly', *Worlding Public*

Cultures <https://www.worldingcultures.org/gatherings/amsterdam-assembly> [both accessed 28 February 2024]. The members of Lakoat.Kujawas who were present during the Amsterdam Assembly (via Zoom and video recording) were Dicky Senda, Toni Oematan, and the representatives of the *To the Lighthouse* writing class, which includes Carmelita Seran, Rhy Bessy, Sandra Liu, and Lauren Tapatab. Lakoat.Kujawas's talk, 'Stories from Kap Na'm to Fena', was part of the *Listening: Building Together Many Voices* session in the Amsterdam Assembly. A recording of the session is available. See, 'Amsterdam Assembly | LISTENING: Building Together Many Voices', YouTube, 8 October 2021 <https://www.youtube.com/watch?v=QlDWDkdE1Gk> [accessed 28 February 2024].

84 See Dicky Senda's Instagram post <https://www.instagram.com/p/CUwB6jTllVD/?hl=en> and Lakoat.Kujawas's Instagram post at the handle @lakoat.kujawas <https://www.instagram.com/p/CUq0UJyh8d5/> [both accessed 10 April 2023].

85 See Ronald Hasudungan Irianto Sitindjak, Laksmi Kusuma Wardani, and Poppy Firtatwentyna Nilasari, 'The Iconography of Sonaf Nis None Traditional House in East Nusa Tenggara, Indonesia', *SHS Web of Conferences*, 76 (2020), pp. 1–11 (p. 7). Also see ibid. to learn more about the structure of the *uem bubu* and the variety of traditional houses in Timor (*sonaf, ume kbubu, lopo, ume kbat/kanaf*). See also Thomas Kurniawan Dima, Antariksa, and Agung Murti Nugroho, 'Konsep Ruang Ume Kbubu Desa Kaenbaun Kabupaten Timor Tengah Utara' (Structure of Ume Kbubu in Kaenbaun Village, North Central Timor), *Jurnal Ruas*, 11.1 (June 2013), pp. 28–36.

86 Anke Niehof, *Food, Diversity, Vulnerability and Social Change: Research Findings from Insular Southeast Asia*, Mansholt Publication Series, 9 (Wageningen: Wageningen Academic Publisher, 2010), p. 97.

87 ALADIN is an abbreviation for Atap (roof), LANtai (roof), and DINding (wall). The Departemen Pemukiman dan Prasarana Wilayah (The Community Housing and Public Infrastructure Department) was in charge of the programme. See Yohanes Kambaru Windi and Andrea Whittaker, 'Indigenous Round Houses versus "Healthy

Houses": Health, Place and Identity Among the Dawan of West Timor, Indonesia', *Health & Place*, 18 (2012), pp. 1153–61 (p. 1157).

88 Ibid., p. 1155.

89 See Semiarto Aja Purwanto and Indraini Hapsari, 'The Story of Building Healthful Houses in East Nusa Tenggara, Indonesia', *Saúde e Sociedade*, 27.2 (2018), pp. 605–14 (pp. 611–12).

90 Windy Ariestanty, 'Lakoat.Kujawas: Masyarakat Adat Mollo Melawan Pemiskinan Negara Indonesia' [Lakoat.Kujawas: Mollo Indigenous Community Against the Impoverishment of the State], *Project Multatuli* (2022) <https://projectmultatuli.org/lakoat-kujawas-masyarakat-adat-mollo-melawan-pemiskinan-negara-indonesia/> [accessed 8 January 2022].

91 Read more about *lumbung* practices in the extensive introduction in the handbook for documenta fifteen. See, ruangrupa and Artistic Team 'Lumbung', in *documenta fifteen Handbook*, ed. by Petra Schmidt, Ralf Schlüter, and Pablo Larios (Berlin: Hatte Cantz Verlag, 2022), pp. 8–43.

REFERENCES

Amiruddin Al Rahab, *Ekonomi Berdikari Sukarno* [Sukarno's Berdikari Economy] (Jakarta: Komunitas Bambu, 2014)
Anderson, Benedict, *Imagined Communities: Reflections on the Origin and Spread of Nationalism* (London and New York: Verso, 2006)
—— *The Spectre of Comparisons: Nationalism, Southeast Asia and the World* (London: Verso, 1998)
Barker, Joshua, and others, 'Figures of Indonesian Modernity', *Indonesia*, 87 (2009), pp. 35–72
Basu, Paul, 'Object Diasporas, Resourcing Communities: Sierra Leonean Collections in the Global Museumscape', *Museum Anthropology*, 34.1 (2011), pp. 28–42
Boast, Robin, 'Neocolonial Collaboration: Museum as Contact Zone Revisited', *Museum Anthropology*, 34.1 (2011), pp. 56–70
British Council, 'Social Innovation in South East Asia Programme, Case Studies Series: Active Citizens in Universities and Communities' (April 2021) <https://www.britishcouncil.org/sites/default/files/sharing_values_and_visions_for_social_change_sisea_case_study_4.pdf> [accessed 24 March 2022]
Clifford, James, 'Museums as Contact Zones', in *Routes: Travel and Translation in the Late Twentieth Century*, ed. by James Clifford (Cambridge, MA: Harvard University Press, 1997), pp. 188–219
Dharmaningtyas, *Pulung Gantung: Menyingkap Tragedi Bunuh Diri di Gunungkidul* [Pulung Gantung: Revealing Suicide Tragedies in Gunungkidul] (Yogyakarta: Salwa Press, 2002)

Diah Widuretno, 'Belajar dari Gaber, Atasi Ancaman Krisis Pangan Pandemi Corona' [Learning from *Gaber*, in Dealing with Food Crisis amidst Corona Pandemic], *Historead*, 25 June 2021 <https://web.archive.org/web/20210921074950/https://historead.co.id/belajar-dari-gaber-atasi-ancaman-krisis-pangan-pandemi-corona/> [accessed 2 February 2022]

—— 'Belajar Mengamankan Pangan dari Masyarakat Wintaos, Gunungkidul' [Learning to Secure Food from Wintaos, Gunungkidul], *Mojok*, 11 May 2023 <https://mojok.co/podium/belajar-mengamankan-pangan-dari-masyarakat-wintaos-gunungkidul/> [accessed 11 May 2023]

—— 'Benih, Pangan dan Kehidupan' [Seed, Food and Life], *Historead*, 1 August 2021 <https://web.archive.org/web/20210921172859/https://historead.co.id/benih-pangan-dan-kehidupan/> [accessed 4 February 2022]

—— *Gesang di Lahan Gersang* [Life in the Barren Land] (Yogyakarta: CV Putra Surya Santosa and Sekolah Pagesangan, 2020)

Doshi, Nishi, 'Calling for "Rematriation": Art, Heritage, and Sovereignty', in *Climate Justice Code for Artists, Art Workers and Art Organisations Situated in the Global North*, ed. by Climate Justice Code Working Group (Utrecht: Casco Art Institute: Working for the Commons, 2023), pp. 81–90

Eko Haryono, Didit Hadi Barianto, and Ahmad Cahyadi, 'Petunjuk Kegiatan Lapangan: Hidrogeologi Kawasan Karst Gunung Sewu' [Field Guide: Hydrogeology of Gunung Sewu Karst Region], in *Pekan Ilmiah Tahunan Perhimpunan Ahli Airtanah Indonesia* [Annual Science Week of the Association of Indonesian Groundwater Specialists], *INA-Rxiv*, 14 September 2017, pp. 1–33 <https://doi.org/10.31227/osf.io/t5dgp>

Escobar, Arturo, *Designs for the Pluriverse: Radical Interdependence, Autonomy, and the Making of Worlds* (Durham, NC: Duke University Press, 2018)

Febriana Firdaus, 'The Battle for the Mountains of Mollo, *The Gecko Project,* 20 November 2020 <https://thegeckoproject.org/articles/the-battle-for-the-mountains-of-mollo/> [accessed 20 March 2021]

Gatari Suryakusuma, 'Pagesangan School: Preserving Food Knowledge in Wintaos Village, Panggang', *Gunung Kidul, Jurnal Bakudapan,* 2 (2019), pp. 78–98

Ghosh, Sanchayan, 'Circl(e)ing Inside Out: Tools for Pedagogy as Art Practice', *March: Journal of Art and Strategy Special Volume: Tools for Radical Study* (2024), ed. by KUNCI Study Forum and Collective, pp. 28–63

Haraway, Donna J., *Staying with the Trouble: Making Kin in the Chthlucene* (Durham, NC: Duke University Press, 2016)

Harney, Stefano, and Fred Moten, *The Undercommons: Fugitive Planning and Black Study* (Wivenhoe, New York: Minor Compositions, 2013)

Harris, Clare, 'Digital Dilemmas: The Ethnographic Museum as Distributive Institution', *Journal of the Anthropological Society of Oxford,* 5.2 (2013), pp. 125–36

Hess, Charlotte, and Elinor Ostrom, 'Introduction: An Overview of the Knowledge Commons', in *Understanding Knowledge as Commons: From Theory to Practice,* ed. by Charlotte Hess and Elinor Ostrom (Cambridge, MA: MIT Press, 2006), pp. 3–26

Hilmar Farid, Razif, 'Batjaan Liar in the Dutch East Indies: A Colonial Antipode', *Postcolonial Studies,* 11.3 (2008), pp. 277–92

Iman Budhi Santosa, and Wage Daksinarga, *Tali Pati: Kisah-kisah Bunuh Diri di Gunung Kidul* [Rope of Death: Stories of Suicide in Gunung Kidul] (Yogyakarta: Jalasutra, 2003)

International Council of Museums, 'Final Report from the Standing Committee for Museum Definition 2022' <https://icom.museum/wp-content/uploads/2022/07/EN_EGA2022_MuseumDefinition_WDoc_Final-2.pdf> [accessed 20 November 2023]

Lee, Doreen, *Activist Archives: Youth Culture and the Political Past in Indonesia* (Durham, NC: Duke University Press, 2016)

Li, Tania Murray, *Land's End: Capitalist Relations on an Indigenous Frontier* (Durham, NC: Duke University Press, 2014)

Maturana, Humberto, and Francisco Varela, *Autopoiesis and Cognition: The Realization of the Living* (Boston, MA: Reidel, 1980)

McKittrick, Katherine, *Dear Science and Other Stories* (Durham, NC: Duke University Press, 2021)

Monica Ndoen, 'Region and Country Report — Indonesia', in *The Indigenous World 2023, 37th Edition*, ed. by Dwayne Mamo, and others (Copenhagen: International Work Group for Indigenous Affairs, 2023), pp. 207–13

Mrazek, Rudolf, *Engineers of Happy Land: Technology and Nationalism in a Colony* (Princeton, NJ: Princeton University Press, 2002)

Mustika Rasa: Resep Masakan Indonesia Warisan Sukarno [Mustika Rasa: Indonesian Cuisine Recipes and Sukarno's Heritage], ed. by JJ Rizal (Jakarta: Komunitas Bambu, 2016)

Niehof, Anke, *Food, Diversity, Vulnerability and Social Change: Research Findings from Insular Southeast Asia*, Mansholt Publication Series, 9 (Wageningen: Wageningen Academic Publisher, 2010)

Nuraini Juliastuti, *Commons People: Managing Music and Culture in Contemporary Yogyakarta* (unpublished doctoral thesis, Leiden University, 2019)

—— '*Sanggar* as a Model for Practicing Art in Communal Life', in *Made in Commons*, ed. by Ferdiansyah Thajib and Kerstin Winking (Amsterdam: Stedelijk Museum Bureau Amsterdam; Yogyakarta: KUNCI Cultural Studies Center, 2013), pp. 9–17

Peers, Laura, and Alison K. Brown, *Museum and Source Communities: A Routledge Reader* (London: Routledge, 2003)

Phillips, Ruth B., 'Introduction: Community Collaborations in Exhibitions: Toward a Dialogic Paradigm', in *Museum and Source Communities*, ed. by Laura Peers and Alison K. Brown (London: Routledge, 2003), pp. 155–70

—— 'Re-Placing Objects: Historical Practices for the Second Museum Age', *Canadian Historical Review*, 86.1 (2005), pp. 83–110

Plunkett, Leo, dir., *Our Mothers' Land* (The Gecko Project and Mongabay, 2020)

Pramoedya Ananta Toer, *Rumah Kaca* [House of Glass] (Jakarta: Lentera Dipantara, 2010)

Resi Nati, and others, *Surat-surat dari Mollo: Sekumpulan Resep dan Cerita* [Letters from Mollo: An Anthology of Recipes and Stories] (Mollo: Lakoat.Kujawas, 2023)

Ronald Hasudungan Irianto Sitindjak, Laksmi Kusuma Wardani, and Poppy Firtatwentyna Nilasari, 'The Iconography of Sonaf Nis None Traditional House in East Nusa Tenggara, Indonesia', *SHS Web of Conferences*, 76 (2020), pp. 1–11 <https://doi.org/10.1051/shsconf/20207601046>

ruangrupa and Artistic Team, 'Lumbung', in *documenta fifteen Handbook*, ed. by Petra Schmidt, Ralf Schlüter, and Pablo Larios (Berlin: Hatje Cantz Verlag, 2022)

Sahid Susanto, 'Mengingat Jaman Gaber' [Remembering Jaman Gaber], *Cerita Fakta Sumberdaya Alam Tropis*, 16 December 2015 <https://ceritafaktasumberdayaalamtropis.tp.ugm.ac.id/index.php/cerita-fakta/cerita-fakta-alam-liar-6/5-mengingat-jaman-gaber> [accessed 12 July 2022]

Semiarto Aja Purwanto, and Indraini Hapsari, 'The Story of Building Healthful Houses in East Nusa Tenggara, Indonesia', *Saúde e Sociedade*, 27.2 (2018), pp. 605–14

Siti Maimunah, *Weaving, Guardian of Identity: Weaving, the Commons and Womanhood* (Jakarta: Poros Photo, Perhimpunan LAWE, Organisasi Attaemamus and GEF-SGP, 2017)

Sumber Sejarah Lisan Revolusi Hijau di Indonesia [Sources of Oral Histories on Green Revolution in Indonesia], ed. by Mona Lohanda (Jakarta: Kementerian Pendidikan dan Kebudayaan Republik Indonesia, 2017)

Thomas Kurniawan Dima, Antariksa, and Agung Murti Nugroho, 'Konsep Ruang Ume Kbubu Desa Kaenbaun Kabupaten Timor Tengah Utara' [Structure of Ume Kbubu in Kaenbaun Village, North Central Timor], *Jurnal Ruas*, 11.1 (June 2013), pp. 28–36

Tsing, Anna Lowenhaupt, *Friction: An Ethnography of Global Connection* (Princeton, NJ: Princeton University Press, 2005)

Tsuchiya, Kenji, 'The Taman Siswa Movement — Its Early Eight Years and Javanese Background', *Journal of Southeast Asian Studies*, 6.2 (1975), pp. 164–77

Tsuchiya, Kenji, and Peter Hawkes, *Democracy and Leadership: The Rise of the Taman Siswa Movement in Indonesia* (Honolulu: University of Hawai'i Press, 1987)

Tuck, Eve, 'Rematriating Curriculum Studies', *Journal of Curriculum and Pedagogy*, 8.1 (2011), pp. 34–37

Tuhiwai Smith, Linda, *Decolonizing Methodologies: Research and Indigenous Peoples* (London: Zed Books; Dunedin: University of Otago Press, 1999)

van Klinken, Gerry, *The Making of Middle Indonesia: Middle Classes in Kupang Town*, 1930s–1980s (Leiden: Brill, 2014)

Windy Ariestanty, '*Lakoat.Kujawas: Masyarakat Adat Mollo Melawan Pemiskinan Negara Indonesia*' [Lakoat.Kujawas: Mollo Indigenous Community Against the Impoverishment of the State], *Project Multatuli* (2022) <https://projectmultatuli.org/lakoat-kujawas-masyarakat-adat-mollo-melawan-pemiskinan-negara-indonesia/> [accessed 8 January 2022]

Yohanes Kambaru Windi, and Andrea Whittaker, 'Indigenous Round Houses versus "Healthy Houses": Health, Place and Identity Among the Dawan of West Timor, Indonesia', *Health & Place*, 18 (2012), pp. 1153–61 <https://doi.org/10.1016/j.healthplace.2012.03.008>

Yunita Khusnul Khotimah, Suprapti Supardi, and Ernoiz Antriyandarti, 'Pemanfaatan Sumber Daya Pertanian Lahan

Kering di Pegunungan Karst Gunung Kidul' [The Utilization of Agricultural Resources in the Drylands in the Gunung Kidul Karst Mountain], in *Seminar Nasional Sumber Daya Pertanian Berkelanjutan dalam Mendukung Ketahanan dan Keamanan Pangan Indonesia pada Era Revolusi Industri 4.0* [Sustainable Agricultural Resources in Supporting Food Resiliency and Security in Indonesia during Industrial Revolution Era 4.0], *Prosiding Seminar Nasional Fakultas Pertanian*, 3.1 (2019), pp. 50–57

Worlding Public Cultures

Series Editor
    Ming Tiampo

Managing Editor
    Eva Bentcheva

Assistant Managing Editor
    Franziska Kaun

Copy Editor
    Francesca Simkin

Editorial Board
    Eva Bentcheva
    May Chew
    Chiara de Cesari
    Birgit Hopfener
    Paul Goodwin
    Alice Ming Wai Jim
    Monica Juneja
    Franziska Koch
    Wayne Modest
    Miriam Oesterreich
    Édith-Anne Pageot
    Ming Tiampo
    Maribel Hildago Urbaneja
    Toshio Watanabe

The publication series takes as its starting point 'Worlding Public Cultures: The Arts and Social Innovation' (WPC), a collaborative research project and transnational platform conceived by the Transnational and Transcultural Arts and Culture Exchange (TrACE) network in 2018.

WPC is funded by the Trans-Atlantic Platform for the Social Sciences and Humanities (T-AP) through a collaboration between the following granting agencies:

> Dutch Research Council (NWO), Netherlands
> Economic and Social Research Council (ESRC), UK
> Federal Ministry of Education and Research (BMBF)/DLR Project Management Agency, Germany
> Fonds de recherche du Québec — Société et culture (FRQSC), Canada
> Social Sciences and Humanities Research Council (SSHRC), Canada

The WPC publication series is produced through the generous funding of ICI Berlin Institute for Cultural Inquiry, BMBF, NWO, FRQSC, SSHRC, and the National Museum of World Cultures, Netherlands.

REGISTERS IN THE SERIES
Troubling Public Cultures: Case Studies
These single and collaboratively-authored Case Studies explore 'worlding' in different regional, temporal, thematic, institutional, and practice-related contexts.

Worlding Concepts
Worlding Concepts serves as a lexicon of key terminology discussed and developed throughout the WPC project.

Academies
These edited volumes present contributions and discussions from WPC academies and assemblies.

Companions for Thinking and Doing
Companions distil the theoretical insights of the WPC project to provide practice-based reflections, proposals, and questions.

List of published titles at: https://doi.org/10.25620/wpc-print.

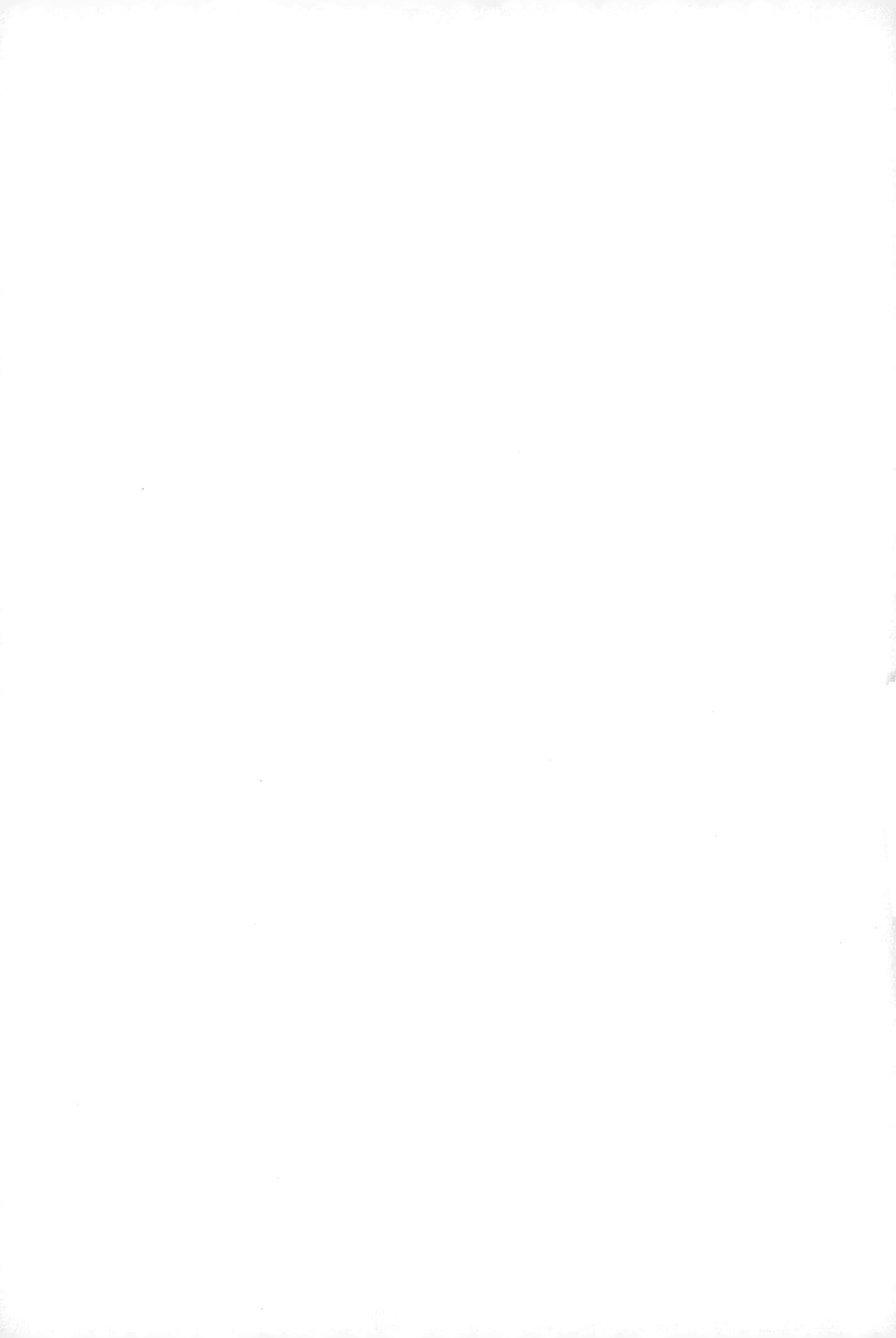

9 783965 580701